GREAT SPACES LEARNING PLACES

BY JAN HUBBARD

CREATIVE ENVIRONMENTS FOR CHILDREN'S MINISTRY

Building the New Generation of Believers

An Imprint of Cook Communications Ministries • Colorado Springs, CO

COLORADO SPRINGS, COLORADO • PARIS, ONTARIO
KINGSWAY COMMUNICATIONS, LTD., EASTBOURNE, ENGLAND

Dedicated to the special blessings in my life:
daughter Amy, son Chad and grandson Aiden.

Thank you for teaching me so much about love.

NexGen® is an imprint of
Cook Communications Ministries, Colorado Springs, CO 80918
Cook Communications, Paris, Ontario
Kingsway Communications, Eastbourne, England

GREAT SPACES, LEARNING PLACES
Creative Environments for Children's Ministry
Copyright © 2005 Cook Communications Ministries

All rights reserved. No part of this book may be reproduced in any manner whatsoever without prior written permission from the publisher, except where noted on handouts and the case of brief quotations embodied in critical articles and reviews. For information write to Permissions Editor, Cook Communications Ministries, 4050 Lee Vance View, Colorado Springs, Colorado 80918.

Authors: Jan Hubbard, Dale Olsen
Editor: Lois Keffer
Art Direction: Nancy L. Haskins
Cover Design: Jeff Barnes, Helen Harrison
Interior Design: Helen Harrison
Cover photos: Lois Keffer

Printed in the United States of America
First printing, 2005
12345678910   07 06 05

ISBN 0781442265

Scripture quotations, unless otherwise noted, are from The Holy Bible: New International Version® (NIV) Copyright © 1973, 1978, 1984 by International Bible Society. Used by permission of Zondervan Publishing House. All rights reserved.

Contents

Chapter 1
Kid-Friendly Spaces
What draws children to Sunday school and helps them retain important Bible lessons? Catch the vision for how experiential learning environments are changing the face of Sunday school—and children's lives! 9

Chapter 2
Interior Design—The Hidden Aspect of Curriculum
Brain studies show that room design makes a significant impact on how children learn. Discover how to revitalize Sunday school with enriched environments that move hearts and minds. 19

Chapter 3
The Creativity Factor—Prime the Pump
Discover the physiology of your creative "muscles." Learn how to bring out each team member's God-given creativity as you begin to build your vision together. Explore the value of hiring a design professional to help in the complex work of creating a new Sunday school space. 29

Chapter 4
Planning Your New Design
Chart your road by gathering information about your church facility, looking at your space with fresh eyes, and writing a strategic plan to bring your dream to fruition. Themes, schemes and dreams…what will your focus be? 39

Chapter 5
Design Development—It's All in the Details
Here's your crash course in design. Move step-by-step through the planning process as the details of your wonderful new ministry space begin to unfold. 53

Chapter 6
Fun Ways with Walls and Ceilings
Stunning effects with faux painting and wallpaper are easier than you imagine, even for first-timers. Get the basics for several techniques and a guide to other great resources. 71

Chapter 7
Structural Savvy—Safe and Up to Code
Safety first! Learn how to unravel the mysteries of building codes, temperature control, fire retardancy, plumbing, ergonomics, lighting, acoustics and indoor air quality. 87

Chapter 8
Work Your Plan
You're ready to roll. Here are the how-tos you'll need to make your vision a reality. Learn how to raise funds, recruit volunteers and organize the tasks ahead. Your hard work is about to pay off! 95

Chapter 9
Jubilee! Celebration and Evaluation
Celebrate your hard work with a special thank you and dedication party involving all the volunteers. Plan your grand opening, then welcome adults to an open house. Evaluate and tweak your design to keep it fresh and functional. 103

Appendix
Meet the Authors,
look through room layouts, drawings for murals and multiple-use cabinets. Order building plans for innovative storage units and the market cart, game board and loft designs you'll see throughout these pages. 109

Foreword

As Children's Pastor at The Village Presbyterian Church in Northbrook, Illinois, I was privileged to have Jan Hubbard on my Children's Ministries Committee when we started exploring new directions for Sunday School. I was amazed not only by her creativity, but by her knowledge of educational issues and her gifts of organization and administration.

In just a few weeks Jan grabbed a hold of the concept of multidimensional learning and drew up the most wonderful designs for our new children's ministries space, "The Kingdom." She worked with the entire committee night after night and even until the wee hours of the morning before our grand opening. We watched the eyes of the children who entered "The Kingdom" at The Village Church that Sunday in September and we cried together out of exhaustion and joy. We asked each other, "Wouldn't it be great if we could do this for other churches?" never dreaming that it would be God's design for us to do just that.

When my colleagues and I began to holding workshops about multidimensional learning, it was only natural that we included Jan. I'll never forget putting a title to her first workshop: "Room Design: The Forgotten Aspect of Curriculum." In 1999 when Children's Ministries of America was officially formed as an organization, Jan was the Secretary of the Board of Directors. Her expertise in transition planning and administration was instrumental in perpetuating this model of Christian education as well as structuring the business plan for the training and event planning organization that has now become Lord and King Associates, Inc.

Jan and I are friends, colleagues and most importantly, sisters in Christ. We have spent hours praying together and I am thrilled that her faith and giftedness have found expression in helping churches release their artistic talents and redesign their classroom space so that children can learn through the rooms themselves as well as the teaching material. How well I remember the child who, upon entering the new Sunday school space, threw her arms open wide and exclaimed, "It's like a whole new world!"

Thank you, Jan. We know that this book will help pastors and educators everywhere see that design is no longer the forgotten aspect of curriculum, but a powerful tool to help children come to know the God who loves them.

Mickie O'Donnell
President, Lord and King Associates, Inc.
Executive Director of the CMA
National Conference on Multidimensional Learning

Introduction

My first venture into the exciting world of designing creative environments for children's ministry began in April of 1996. I was attending The Village Presbyterian Church in Northbrook, Illinois, serving on the Children's Ministries Committee. At that time, Mickie O'Donnell was Director of Children's Ministry. She explained to us a marvelous new model for children's ministry known as Workshop Rotation/Multidimensional Learning. In this model, children would rotate to different workshop rooms each week. In each location they approached the Bible story using different media that would stimulate all eight "intelligences." Remaining with the same story for four to five weeks and exploring Bible truths through storytelling, science or cooking, art projects, video, lively games, drama and puppetry caused the Bible truths to take root in children's minds and hearts.

I caught the vision! Our church decided to move ahead with this model and I became the Interior Designer. We chose to call our new children's ministry area "The Kingdom." In a brainstorming session we developed word pictures of our concepts, listed all the workshops we wanted to include and pored over curriculum ideas. That night I sat at my drafting table drawing rough sketches of window treatments, signage, furnishings and color ideas for the work stations in our open floor plan. I named each workshop with creative, descriptive titles such as "Puppet Paradise" and "Mega Memory Street."

Then the construction began. Because our plan called for major revamping of a large area, we began by tearing out the interior walls of the third floor. In the following six months we poured our creativity into "The Kingdom." With the help of volunteers from our congregation we carpeted, painted, upgraded lighting, furnished and decorated.

As with any remodeling project, we dealt with our share of unforeseen problems, hard physical work and unexpected delays. In spite of these inevitable challenges, our team found the process to be great creative fun. Conquering each part of the project brought a rush of exhilaration. And in the end, it was one of the most fulfilling experiences of our lives.

The long-anticipated opening of "The Kingdom" came on a bright September Sunday morning. It was amazing to see the children's delight as they ran in to see the new Sunday school they'd been hearing so much about. They responded in wide-eyed wonder. Tears came to my eyes as I watched them dive into the exciting learning experiences offered at each workshop. As we saw first-hand how the children responded with new enthusiasm for studying God's Word, an old hymn came to mind: "I love to tell the story, because I know it's true…"

Our church was one of the first in this new Workshop Rotation /Multidimensional Learning Model for Christian education. Thrilled with the results I was seeing at my own church, I joined a network of Chicago area Christian educators who supported each other in using this model and shared their expertise with other churches. I began conducting workshops on interior design at the annual National Workshop Rotation Model Conferences. I have since worked with churches around the country to develop Sunday school environments for both self-contained classrooms and workshop rotation rooms.

Though I have run a thriving residential interior design firm for years, my work with churches has given me a wealth of specialized information about tackling projects for this unique setting. I care deeply about children's early experiences of God and understand the specific challenges involved in creating fresh, enriched church school environments where children can develop a life-long love for God's Word. So I've compiled into this book both the principles of design I can offer as a professional and the invaluable lessons on working within church settings that only experience can provide.

I hope that within these pages you'll find inspiration and encouragement to bring to your children's ministry the excitement, joy and depth of learning that enriched environments can offer.

Blessings,

Jan Hubbard

Chapter One
Kid-Friendly Spaces

"Our attendance has increased to the tune of 20%. We've had a lot of people who had quit coming to church come back. They had said it was hard to get the kids out of bed, it was hard to interest them in coming to church. Now the parents are no longer having to fight that battle."
—Nita Gilger, Minister of Christian Education, University Christian Church, Fort Worth, TX

Sunday School is about making memories. Memories of life-changing encounters with God's Word. Of taking the first steps in being a follower of Jesus. Of happy times with caring teachers. We want the precious hours children spend in Sunday School to be engraved on their hearts and minds as a touchstone that will shape their future relationships with God and his people.

Kid-Friendly Spaces page 9

What Makes a Memory?

Think about your most vivid memories from childhood. What comes to mind? I think of family vacations. The dock where I dangled my toes in the water, the old row-boat where I learned to fish, the smoky campfires where we made s'mores and the sweet, toasted stickiness dripping down my chin. These things are etched so indelibly in my mind that I can almost reach out and touch them.

- TOUCH wriggling fish; soft, comfy beach towels

- TASTE sweet gooey marshmallows; salty chips

- SMELL lake water; pungent pine branches

- SEE star-spangled night sky; murky green underwater light

- HEAR crickets; the creek and bang of a screen door

I remember swimming in the lake and coming out with a leech on each toe. Mom called Dad and he carefully removed them. There was the carefree feeling of living all day in my swim suit, smelling like water, and feeling the scorch on my skin by dinnertime. I can feel the cool trickle of an evening shower and utter contentment of staying up late and stargazing in my pajamas.

Why are these particular memories so tangible and accessible? Because these experiences touched all my senses.

Are you there with me?

The lakeside setting was out of the ordinary. It was something beyond the backyard swing set, my familiar room with its parade of stuffed animals or my school with institutional green walls and buzzing fluorescent lights. The lake was special.

Make Sunday School Special!

Sunday school needs to be a special place with intriguing sights, smells, tastes, sounds. A place where children experience the Bible through every avenue to their minds. A place they will remember.

Perhaps you've heard the expression, "travel is the best education." It's hard to connect words and dates in a history book to real people—their families, their feelings, their world. But a visit to Williamsburg gives the Colonial period a living, breathing context. A walk across the green battlefields of the Civil War evokes a sense of solemn respect. A reconstructed 1800's town high in the Rocky Mountains puts the hardships of the pioneer life in sharp perspective. And settling on a cushion by a low table in a room that replicates an Israelite home allows children to "travel" back to Bible times and experience the richness of God's story.

In a well designed children's ministry area, kids may travel down a hallway decorated with a camel caravan. They pass by an ancient marketplace complete with striped awnings and a cart with fruit and vegetables. Their escorts are robed shepherds who greet them with a friendly "Shalom!" Mary visits the room and tells the children what it was like when Jesus was born—the wondrous, frightening visit from the angel, the long, dusty road to Bethlehem, the crowded little town with no rooms, the quiet refuge of the stable, the wonder of holding the tiny Christ child. Suddenly the story lives and breathes. And children will never forget it.

This is why we deck the halls and paint the walls—to give kids a fascinating environment where God's ancient story becomes new and memorable.

We give them more than facts. We give them experiences.

Kid-Friendly Spaces

"These commandments that I give you today are to be upon your hearts. Impress them on your children. Talk about them when you sit at home and when you walk along the road, when you lie down and when you get up. Tie them as symbols on your hands and bind them on your foreheads. Write them on the doorframes of your houses and on your gates."
—Deuteronomy 6:6-9

This passage gives a wonderful description of experiential learning. God didn't want his words to be forgotten. So he told the people to teach their children during all their life experiences—sitting, walking, lying down, rising. "Book learning" was never God's ideal for teaching his truth. He knew that words of Scripture need to be interwoven with life experiences. In multidimensional learning, our goal is to create events in stimulating environments where children experience the Bible with their minds, their senses and their emotions.

The past twenty years of brain research has given us new insights into how children learn. Experience becomes even more important when an emotion is

attached to it. Emotions are like little flags in our minds that say, "Hey—remember this!" They tag our experiences and embed them deeply in long-term memory. Living out Bible stories in Bible-time settings with costumed characters delivering the stories allows children to feel the joy of a healed leper, the sadness of a grieving mother, the fear of fishermen floundering in storm-tossed sea, the wonder at an angel's appearance, the contentment of a seaside afternoon in Jesus' company. Enriched environments set the stage for learning that sticks.

Historically in the church we've designed children's spaces like traditional school classrooms. There's a central table, chairs and a few supplies. Décor amounts to the teacher's ability to create bulletin boards, display teaching pictures and put up children's art. The typical church classroom looks like a miniature boardroom where children sit, listen, read and write. Whoa! It's time to step back and reassess what we're about here: making memories through experiences. Listening, reading and writing are great for a certain percentage of our kids. But the majority of them need to move, interact, squish clay between their fingers, perform a drama or puppet show, cook up a story-enhancing treat or create an artistic masterpiece that expresses what they've learned from the Bible story. Enhanced learning environments *invite* that kind of activity. Bible lessons go from "Ho-hum" to "Hey—wow!"

What's Behind the Change?

A significant culture shift drives this innovative approach to teaching. Traditional classrooms were designed for use in the Industrial Era. Now we're living in the Information Age. Look at some of the differences.

Industrial Era

- kids as listeners
- lecture based
- standard textbooks
- competition in the classroom
- teacher is front and center
- lockstep classes

Information Age

- kids as explorers
- discovery based
- multimedia learning
- cooperative learning
- teacher is a guide
- individual goals

The Information Era has a great effect on us all. It can be fast-paced and overwhelm. It also provides us with opportunities to connect with people around the world in real time, have "virtual experiences," and bring up information in a matter of seconds in our quest for knowledge.

Remember the days of poring over heavy reference books at the library and writing meticulous note cards in preparation for a report? That world is long gone. Kids have information at their fingertips. Imagine how we can use that resource in church. What did the walls of Jericho look like? How far did Mary and Joseph have to travel to reach Bethlehem from Nazareth? What causes vicious storms to brew on the Sea of Galilee? When Jesus mentioned "the lilies of the field," what kinds of flowers might he have been looking at? How exciting for kids to come up with their own questions about Bible stories and Bible culture, then navigate the Internet to find the answers! That kind of learning is light years from printed fill-in-the blank questions.

- How will this science experiment turn out and what will it help me understand about the Bible story?

- I wonder which Bible character I'll get to be today.

- I could never sit still today—I'm so glad we're going to the game room!

- Today's Bible verse helped me see something I never understood before—I can't wait to write it down in my journal.

- I've heard this story a zillion times, but now I really get it!

In Search of Truth

With multidimensional learning, kids are no longer listeners—they're explorers! With their own curiosity as guide, delving into the Bible becomes a fascinating experience.

The computer lab, the game room, the theater, the art studio, the science and cooking lab, the music room. All these places invite children to dig in, explore, experience and learn. In fact, they can't wait to charge in and find out what fascinating tasks await them each week.

If you've never visited a workshop rotation/multidimensional learning Sunday school, take a week and do so. See for yourself the kind of return you can expect from your investment in kid-friendly rooms.

Great Spaces—Learning Places

Beyond "Pretty"

Our new designs must capture kids' attention, soothe their stress, stimulate their natural curiosity. Then we teachers follow up with the all-important connection to life that tranforms information into changed lives. Enriched environments do that, not only for the kids but for the adults who guide the experiences.

Suppose you had the choice of these settings for telling the Bible story: a room with standard church-beige paint and chairs around a central table, or a Bible time inn where children sit on cushions around a low table amidst pottery, oil lamps, richly colored rugs and Bible land scenes peeking through faux windows? If the latter scene excites you, imagine a child's reaction!

Well planned rooms fire kids' imaginations and stoke their desire to understand the world of the Bible. The design behind our designs isn't about making things pretty. It's about investing in environments that move hearts and minds.

Kid-Friendly Spaces

We have THE most important lessons for kids to learn, and one hour a week to teach them. We want to give them the joy of discovering God's Word through all the pathways to the mind. Our goal isn't just information transfer—it's changed lives! You'll find that the time and resources you invest in creating multidimensional learning environments will come back to you a hundred fold.

A Place of Refuge

Think about the constant media rush that confronts kids every day. Conservative estimates state that kids watch an average of 21 hours of television a week. In many homes, the TV is left on most of the time. Hours in front of the TV are augmented by more hours video gaming. The radio rattles and pulses in the car. No wonder kids get to church overstimulated and distracted.

Childhood depression and stress are growing concerns across our country. Many factors contribute to this trend. Children fear the breakup of their families. The secure base of extended family has dissipated, leaving kids "on their own" more and more. Add violence on TV, fear of disaster, over-involvement in activities and high expectations from parents and you get an overwhelming mix that forces kids to grow up too fast.

Because we're dealing with kids who are wired, stressed and depressed, we need to focus our children's ministries on being places of refuge. We want to create spaces that appeal to kids without overwhelming them. Room environments can help kids focus on a certain task. Depending on the purpose of the room, you may want a calming environment that encourages thoughtful introspection, or a room that immediately centers kids' attention on art or drama. The chapters that follow will give you insights into how to create just the right atmosphere for caring adults to lead kids toward a life-changing knowledge of our loving God.

Room environments can help kids focus on a certain task.

Beyond Entertainment

Some folks confuse enriched learning environments with fun and entertainment. There's absolutely nothing wrong with kids having fun as they learn, but it's

page 16　Great Spaces—Learning Places

important to realize that great children's ministry environments are *not* about entertainment. Entertainment design focuses on the design rather than tying in to learning. A large cartoon character, for example, is very entertaining but can be distracting. Kids are already distracted! They need rooms that will help them focus on particular learning tasks.

Kid-friendly spaces vary in their intent. An art room with easels, attractively stored supplies, displays of student art, good lighting and a stack of art references immediately draws kids to the task at hand. A computer room needs comfortable seating, lighting that won't cause glare on the screens and a focus on technology. Storytelling rooms need to be cozy and home-like, whether they portray a tent, a Bible-time home or an inn.

As you begin the design process, create rooms that are deliberate in their purpose and will help children focus on the activity at hand. Some will be exciting and stimulating. Others will be calming, inviting thoughtful conversation and introspection. They are child-sized, child-themed and child-safe.

Getting from "here to there" is a five-step process.

- *Planning*
- *Creative Concept*
- *Develop the Design*
- *Work Your Plan*
- *Celebrate and Evaluate*

From Here to There

Perhaps you're thinking this all sounds wonderful, but the task of getting from where you are to where you'd like to be seems overwhelming, maybe even unattainable. Take heart. This book will walk you through the process step by step. Many churches have created wonderful learning environments with limited resources. So can you!

Kid-Friendly Spaces

The following chapters will lead you through each of these five steps and set you up with a project notebook to help you organize it all. This is not a "just add water" process or a turn-key operation. There's definitely a sweat factor involved here! But this book gives you the benefit of years of professional experience in many different churches. With these how-tos and the help of the handy-man/handy-ma'am in your church, you will be on your way to bringing quality space to your children's program.

"Mom, why didn't you do this when I was in Sunday school?"
—My own children, Chad, age 29,
and Amy, age 23

Chapter Two

Interior Design—The Hidden Aspect of Curriculum

"Solomon covered the inside of the temple with pure gold, and he extended gold chains across the front of the inner sanctuary, which was overlaid with gold... He placed the cherubim inside the innermost room of the temple, with their wings spread out. The wing of one cherub touched one wall, while the wing of the other touched the other wall, and their wings touched each other in the middle of the room... On the walls all round the temple, in both the inner and outer rooms, he carved cherubim, palm trees and open flowers. He also covered the floors of both the inner and outer rooms of the temple with gold."

—1 Kings 6:21, 27, 29-30

Solomon constructed the magnificent temple in Jerusalem to reflect the glory of God. Soaring columns, carved cedar paneling, the finest stonework and overlays of pure gold—everything about the temple reflected God's sovereign majesty. Its magnificence drew people's thoughts from everyday concerns and helped them focus on worship. And worship was no odious task, but a time of deep joy. Solomon's father David wrote,

"I rejoiced with those who said to me, "Let us go to the house of the Lord."

—Psalm 122:1

God gave his people a marvelous visual experience each time they approached the gleaming building atop the Temple Mount. While knowing God is a spiritual experience, what we take in with our senses contributes to what we come to know in our hearts and minds. What and how we teach our kids about God is of paramount importance to their journeys as young disciples. WHERE we teach is significant as well.

Space Makes a Difference

Educators have caught on to the role of environment in learning. Large corporations and national conferences dedicate themselves to creating optimal learning spaces in our increasingly competitive world.

"The factors responsible for student achievement are ecological. They act together as a whole in shaping the context within which learning takes place. The physical setting—the school building—is an undeniably integral part of this ecological context for learning."
—Jeffery Lackney, PhD, AIA
Director, School Design Research Studio

The wisest teachers know that one well planned room will not be all things to all students. Think about your own learning habits. Do you study to music? Can you block background chatter, or do you need quiet? Do you prefer to sit at a desk or sprawl in an easy chair? Can you put up with fluorescent light, or do you prefer the warmth of incandescent bulbs? Does bright sunlight help you or make you nuts? What about temperature—do you need it a little chilly to stay alert or do you prefer to be warm and cozy? Does munching help you get through a learning task?

As an adult, you can control most of these environmental factors. Kids, however, seldom have a choice. Their physical situation has a tremendous impact on what they're able to take in and retain. Having a variety of well-planned environments means every child will hit his or her optimum situation some of the time.

Meeting Needs

A hundred years ago kids felt fortunate to have a one-room schoolhouse within twenty miles. (And old-timers will tell you it was uphill both ways!) Have you ever had the privilege of visiting a hundred-year-old schoolhouse? Books with tiny print were treasured and shared by all. Even in bitter winter temperatures a single stove at the center of the room provided the only heat. Boys' and girls' outhouses stood at the back. One-room schools were lucky to have a flag, a map of the United States and the world, a portrait of the president and a clock. Pegs hung at the back of the room for coats and lunch pails. Discipline was administered with the painful, welt-raising smack of a ruler on open palms.

A small percentage of students went on to pursue higher education. The purpose of those early schools was to give children the basic life skills needed to run a farm or a business. School schedules gave way to the needs of the family farm, epidemics of influenza and bouts of severe weather. Yet, children in those one-room schools knew that a free public education was a gift that had not long been available to every class of people.

In the late 1700s, there was no education for child laborers in England. They worked six long days a week, many as chimney sweeps still small enough to scramble up the dark, sooty confines of a clogged flue. These children had no way to improve their situation. Gangs of them would roam the streets and cause trouble on Sunday, their one day off. Newspaper editor Robert Raikes began the "Sunday school" movement as an outreach to these child laborers. Raikes knew from his experience with prison inmates what kinds of lives lay in store for these young troublemakers if someone didn't intervene. His Sunday school gave them a safe, warm place off the streets where they learned to read, cipher and understand the basics of God's Word. By the mid-1780s, the Sunday school movement surged across England.

Teacher and philanthropist Hannah More continued and expanded the practice in the 1800s. In her booklet, "Hints On How to Run a Sunday School," she offered several principles that we commonly practice in our Sunday school programs today. She advised:

- plan programs suited to the level of the students
- offer variety
- make classes as entertaining as possible
- use singing when energy and attention is waning
- it's possible to get the best out of children if their affections are "engaged by kindness"
- terror does not pay
- give small rewards for regular attendance and learning Scripture.[1]

Today's Issues

Those pioneers in Sunday school were certainly on the right track. They provided basic needs of the children of their time. The children of our time deal with much different issues. They've changed because times have changed. Following the tradition of Sunday school pioneers, we need to be sensitive to providing for the spiritual needs of today's kids. We do not need to stimulate our children. Quite the opposite: we need to calm them.

Children are over-stimulated by computers, internet and television. We have a society of stressed kids following hectic schedules. A growing number of children are on medication. National Mental Health Institute Statistics studies show that one in ten kids have learning/behavioral disabilities and that anxiety disorders are a rapidly growing concern.[2] Enriched environments help teachers to bring kids out of "hyper" mode and allow them to explore God's truth through thoughtfully planned learning experiences.

Great Spaces—Learning Places

Environment and the Brain

Recent discoveries in brain research show us that environment can have a great impact on brain development.

"Environment changes the brain! Enriched environment—increased cell weight, increased branching of dendrites. Impoverished environment—decrease in cell weight, possible loss of cells, dendrites are diminished. What your students do determines the actual physical structure of their brains… how many connections they have and how elaborate and sophisticated their networks are.

What constitutes an enriched environment for students? An environment which is stimulating and challenging and in which the students' minds are actively involved." Pat Wolfe, 1997

Educational studies indicate that we learn in many ways. Howard Gardner has identified eight intelligences that we each possess to varying degrees.[3] They are:

Linguistic-verbal—"word smart" people excel in spoken, read and written language.

Logical-mathematical—"math smart" people exhibit strong ability to use numbers and see logical patterns.

Spatial—"picture smart" people can visualize and show ideas graphically.

Bodily-kinesthetic—"physically smart" people can use their bodies expressively and use their hands to perform complex tasks.

Musical—"music smart" are sensitive to musical forms and can express themselves through music.

Interpersonal/relational—"people smart" people can perceive and respond to what others are thinking.

Intrapersonal/introspective—"self-smart" people understand why they think and act the way they do.

Naturalistic—"nature smart" people demonstrate understanding and skill with aspects of nature such as ecology, plants and animals.

Carefully designed learning environments appeal to all eight intelligences, allowing kids to explore Bible truths using every key pathway to their brains. Our challenge is to create rooms where kids will combine the use of several intelligences as they explore God's Word.

Owned Faith

Kids can listen to a teacher talk about God's Word week after week, year after year. But it is through experience that children come to own their faith. Each Bible-based experience builds faith. Through multiplied experiences, kids find their identity as beloved children of a loving Heavenly Father and brothers and sisters in Christ.

When children use all their senses and all their intelligences to explore, wonder about and celebrate God's love, their faith grows and flourishes.

We retain 90% of what we experience, as compared to a mere 10% of what we hear. What we experience becomes a part of us, deeply rooted in long-term memory. Over time, that embedded knowledge shapes our lives.

It is our senses that make experiences real. And that is why design is so important. We want to create learning environments where children can touch, taste,

"Come, this is your **special place** to learn about God. Delightful experiences await you here."

smell, hear and see things that will expand their understanding of who God is and how much he loves them. When children use all their senses and all their intelligences to explore, wonder about and celebrate God's love, their faith grows and flourishes. Our rooms need to be designed for active participation—not just for listening, talking and writing. A well-designed room beckons children: "Come, this is your special place to learn about God.

Interior Design—The Hidden Aspect of Curriculum

Delightful experiences await you here." Children can't wait to squish their fingers through yeasty dough and smell the heavenly aroma of baking bread as they learn that Jesus said, "I am the bread of life." A room prepared with a stage, a curtain, special lighting and a trunk of costumes invites kids to make Bible stories leap off the page and into dramas where they're the writers and actors. Easels and paints entice, science labs pique curiosity, quiet spaces reminiscent of ancient synagogues issue a silent but compelling call to worship. The physical design of the room is truly an important aspect of curriculum!

Learning from the Pros

When school facilities researchers design education spaces, they focus on these factors:

- lighting (sight)
- clean air (smell)
- acoustics (hearing)
- ergonomics and thermal control (touch)

We need to take these factors into careful account in our church spaces as well. Interior Designers approach their task by meeting these criteria.

- Function: the space works well and serves the needs of its users.
- Structure: it is well made of good materials.
- Aesthetics: it is pleasing to the senses.

page 26 Great Spaces—Learning Places

We use the elements and principles of design to create rooms with excellent function, structure and aesthetics. We'll explore how to apply these tools in later chapters.

American design often is based on merchandising. We decorate a room according to the latest cartoon character or super-hero. That approach is colorful and entertaining, but it doesn't fulfill our goals as Christian educators. In our church designs in churches, we want to:

1. apply good, sound design principles,

2. use materials and elements appropriate for the activity in the space and the children who will be using the space, and

3. make it aesthetically pleasing.

We can borrow further principles for successful learning environments from retailers who specialize in children's spaces.

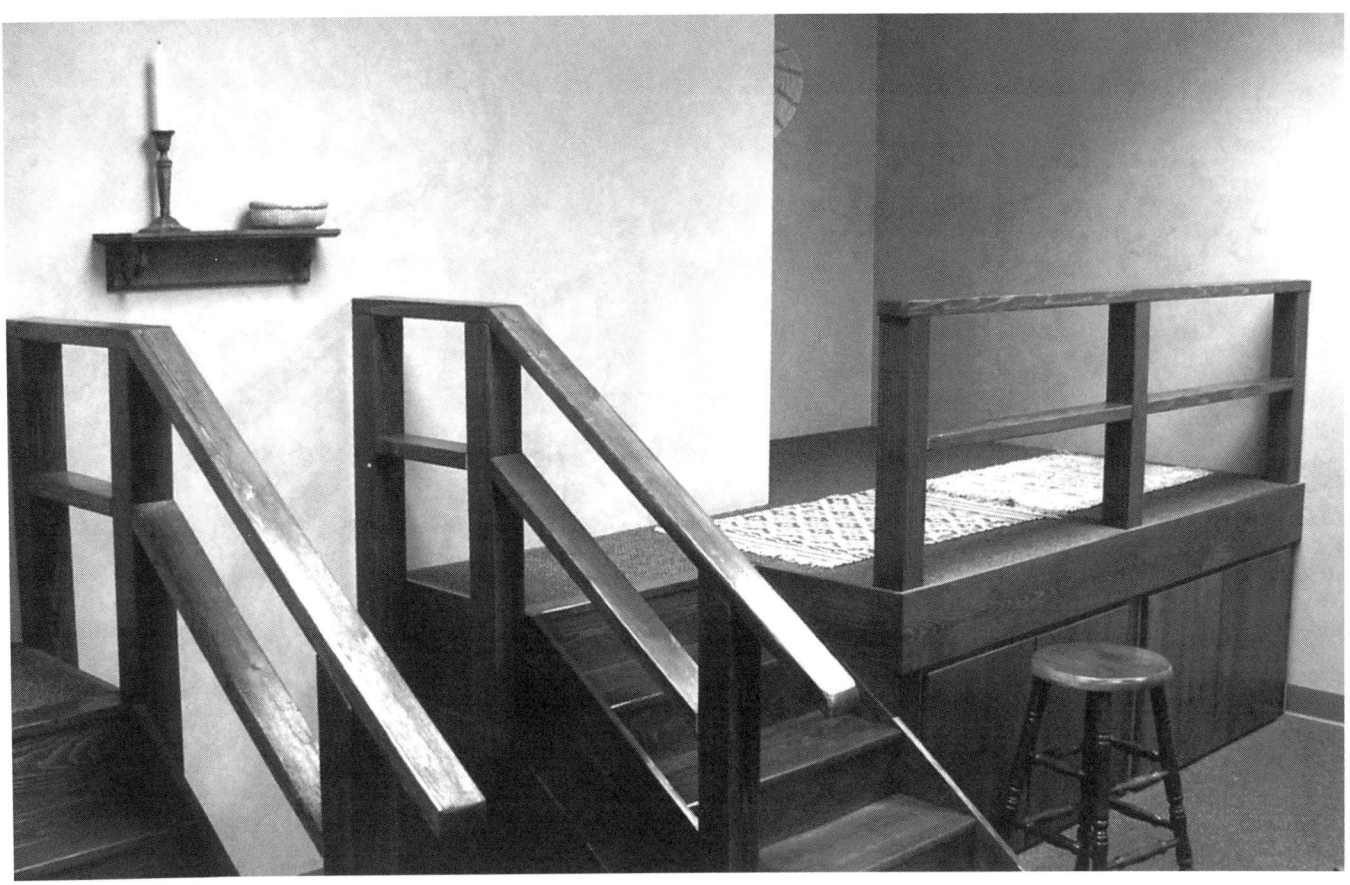

Interior Design—The Hidden Aspect of Curriculum

◩ Create a sense of place that

> Offers playing
>
> Offers listening
>
> Offers touching
>
> Offers learning

◩ Tell a good story

We are about telling God's story—the greatest story ever told! This means choosing the very best Bible-based curriculum to reach the hearts of kids.

◩ Create a brand identity

In the children's ministry world, this means creating a theme that carries through your learning space. Imagery becomes a strong theme of communication.

◩ Build an excellent team

That would be YOU, your staff and volunteers!

◩ The Goal

We want to apply principles and elements of design to provide calm, welcoming places for children in our churches. Thoughtful, creative interior design is an aspect of curriculum that has been overlooked for too long. Join the Sunday school revolution! Create a captivating children's ministry environment that will help the children in your ministry delve deeply into life-changing experiences with God's Word. The chapters that follow will unfold the planning process step by step.

---

1 (from Hannah More: Sunday schools, education and youth work, The Encyclopedia of Informal Education, http://www.infed.org/thinkers/more.html)

2 Mental Health: A Report of the Surgeon General
www.surgeongeneral.gov/library/mentalhealth/chapter3/sec6.html

3 Multiple Intelligences, Howard Gardner, 1993, Basic Books

Chapter Three

The Creativity Factor—Prime the Pump

"He called a little child and had him stand among them. And he said: "I tell you the truth, unless you change and become like little children, you will never enter the kingdom of heaven. Therefore, whoever humbles himself like this child is the greatest in the kingdom of heaven. And whoever welcomes a little child like this in my name welcomes me,"

Matthew 18:2-5

You're about to embark on an amazing creative journey. Rethinking and redesigning your children's ministry will require you and your team to draw deeply from your well of creativity. How is that well—fresh and free-flowing, or just a bit stagnant? Let's get that squeaky pump-handle moving and discover some simple but brilliant ways to prime the pump of creativity.

If you're going to design a space that appeals to children, a first order of business is to find a child-like mindset. Children are fresh from God, not yet shaped and "civilized" by society. They delight us (and sometimes embarrass us!) with their spontaneity. They delighted Jesus as well. From his statement in Matthew 18:5, he intended us to understand that when we welcome children in his name, we're welcoming Jesus himself.

What a context for your redesign work— you're preparing a place to welcome Jesus!

Children had little status in Jesus' time. To let them run around and interfere with a busy rabbi was unthinkable. Jesus' disciples were not being mean-spirited when they shooed the children away. They were simply watching over their rabbi and protecting his teaching time, as any good disciple would do. Jesus used the occasion to teach them a whole new mindset. *These children are precious. Look at their humility, their open hearts, their uncomplicated joy, their simple faith. You have a lot to learn from them.* That must have spun the disciples heads around a few times! And it happened more than once.

"People were bringing little children to Jesus to have him touch them, but the disciples rebuked them. When Jesus saw this, he was indignant. He said to them, 'Let the little children come to me, and do not hinder them, for the kingdom of God belongs to such as these. I tell you the truth, anyone who will not receive the kingdom of God like a little child will never enter it.' And he took the children in his arms, put his hands on them and blessed them." Mark 10:13-16

Great Spaces—Learning Places

When fearful parents of children who were dying or already dead came to Jesus, he healed the children or raised them from the dead. Take comfort from these actions of Jesus: in focusing energy and resources on children, you're doing just as he did. Your priorities are right on.

A Childlike Mindset

This is an opportunity to do a little positive regression (if there can be such a thing!). Sometimes the responsibilities of adult life so bind us that our creative "muscles" get flabby. Cutting lose and letting your brain run freely like a child's can be great fun.

Two beloved children's writers had interesting insights into their own creativity. What can you learn from them?

> "Thank goodness I was never sent to school; it would have rubbed off some of the originality."
> -Beatrix Potter, author of Peter Rabbit

> "One of the advantages of being disorderly is that one is constantly making exciting discoveries."
> -A. A. Milne, author of Winnie the Pooh

Stories from these writers have delighted generations of children. They each recognized that their creativity stemmed in part from being slightly out of the ordinary. Their way of thinking remained fresh, curious and childlike. That's the kind of creativity you need from your design team. Some may shake their heads and say, "But I don't have a creative bone in my body." Your response? "Oh yes you do!"

Our Source

Our creator God made us in his image. We're each blessed with a portion of God's creative nature. It's simply divine! Some tap into that inspiration daily. Others may let it lie dormant for long periods of time. To accomplish the task of creating a mind- and heart-inspiring children's ministry area, a place where you will welcome Jesus and his children, everyone on the team needs to allow God to stir those creative juices that are his gift to us.

> "Creativity is a type of learning process where the teacher and pupil are located in the same individual."
> -Arthur Koestler

As you approach the process, consciously open your mind to God. Ask him to create a flow of ideas and inspiration. Synergy within a lively creative team is one of the most delightful things you'll ever experience. Take into account that the process is guided by the Holy Spirit for use in God's Kingdom, and you're in for a heavenly encounter!

Physiology of Your Creative "Muscles"

When our physical muscles get flabby, toning them involves sweat and pain. Toning our creative "muscles" is a much more pleasant process. We all are creative; it's part of our divine design. Lots of things can cause us to let our creativity fall dormant—crushing schedules, life crises, illness, habit. On the other hand, simple strategies can get the juices flowing again.

Creativity is not a "vision in the middle of the night." It is simply a kernel of thought. It's an idea that pops into your head. When you recognize its potential, you begin to ponder it. As you mull it over, the kernel of thought grows into a full-fledged idea. Intuition is the guide in this process.

Think of that kernel of an idea like a ping-pong ball. As you develop it, the two hemispheres of your brain play ping-pong with it. The right side of your brain imagines and pictures; the logical left side tests and refines.

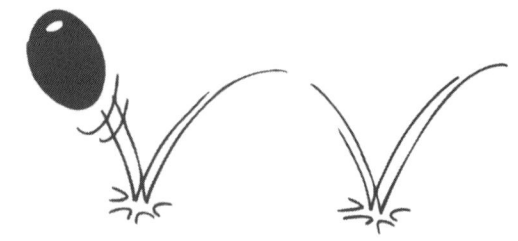

Great Spaces—Learning Places

creativity Boosters

⌑ Be aware of what inspires you.
- ○ walking in the rain
- ○ children at play
- ○ doodling
- ○ your favorite music
- ○ working with your hands
- ○ the fragrance of flowers
- ○ leafing through a magazine

⌑ Notice things with all your senses.
- ○ go through the grocery store backward
- ○ hang off your bed and look at the world upside-down
- ○ laugh when you trip over your words
- ○ add fragrance to your work space
- ○ touch an interesting surface
- ○ walk through your house with your eyes closed

⌑ Enjoy child-like moments.
- ○ ask yourself three "I wonder" questions each day
- ○ read an old favorite children's book
- ○ get down on the floor and play
- ○ learn to juggle
- ○ realize that there's no such thing as a dumb question
- ○ lie on the grass and watch the clouds

⌑ Breathe and know God's presence.

"The Lord God formed the man from the dust of the ground and breathed into his nostrils the breath of life, and the man became a living being." Genesis 2:7

"But it is the spirit in a man, the breath of the Almighty, that gives him understanding." Job 32:8

"The Spirit of God has made me; the breath of the Almighty gives me life." Job 33:4

"Let everything that has breath praise the Lord. Praise the Lord." Psalm 150:6

Permission to photocopy this handout granted for local church use. Copyright © Cook Communications Ministries. Printed in "Great Spaces, Learning Places" by Jan Hubbard.

Your Creative Journey

As a leader in your children's ministry redesign process, you need to learn how to tap into your own creativity. Even more important, you need to help your team members do the same. This may sound as easy as pie. Or, it might have you sighing, shaking your head and questioning your sanity. Never fear. The creative warm-ups that follow will set the tone for fruitful (and fun!) brainstorming sessions.

Assure your team that we never lose our creativity. It does not diminish with age. (How comforting!) There is a learned mindset that quickens our creative sensibilities. Here are some ways to develop that mindset. Photocopy the handout on page 33 and share it with your team members. Tuck it in an envelope, write the team member's name in big, childish letters and tape on a lollipop.

The Creative Profile

In his book, *A Whack on the Side of the Head* (Warner Business Books, 1998), Roger Von Oech describes creative people. Here are just a few of the characteristics he lists:

- Have keen power of observation
- Are sensitive to self and stimuli from outside
- Look for challenge
- Brainstorm well, find solutions
- Are flexible
- Are risk takers
- Think critically but don't get stuck in analyzing

You can find a host of printed and internet resources on creativity. Here are some of my favorites.
- *A Whack on the Side of the Head* by Roger Von Oech (Warner Business Books, 1998)
- *Aha!* by Jordan Ayan (Three Rivers Press, 1997)
- *Jump Start Your Brain* by Doug Hall (Warner Books, 1996)
- GoCreate.com
- CreativeThink.com
- CreativityPortal.com

Inspiring Your Team

Either you have it or you don't—that's how many people think of creativity. But that's not the case! Creativity is a skill that can be developed. Here are some simple strategies to inspire creativity in your children's ministry team.

Don't have meetings—have parties! Start with food and fun every time.

Choose great locations for your meetings. A nearby state park lodge? Someone's family room-with-a-view? Your usual meeting space with an unusual mix of furniture? Be sure to set out beverages and munchies. Have work tables off to the side where people can sketch and doodle. Set out piles of sticky notes and pencils. Set a table or two at the end of the room for spin-off projects or sub-committee meetings. Provide newsprint and markers, white boards, pads and pencils.

Always begin with a quick creativity warm-up to get blood flowing and minds in gear. Here are several examples.

- Write your name with your left hand. Turn your paper over and try to write the mirror image of your name.

- Make yourself as small as you can. Hold for ten seconds. Make yourself as huge as you can; hold for ten seconds. Make yourself look like you don't have any bones and flop into your chair.

- Face a partner. One partner mirrors the other's actions for 30 seconds. Then switch roles.

The Creativity Factor—Prime the Pump

○ Blow soap bubbles and see if you can catch them with the wand before they touch the ground.

○ Sit in a circle and pray for God to bless your creative process. Each person adds one word to the prayer.

○ Line up sheets of paper on the floor. Have the person at one end start a doodle that goes from one side of the paper to the other. He or she hands the marker to the next person who continues the doodle. Keep passing the marker until you have one long doodle. Now go back to the beginning. Trace your doodle with your finger and sing its ups and downs.

Adding Professional Brain Power

Creativity, the ability to brainstorm, then create and work a plan, are key steps in a process that will serve the children of your congregation for years to come. It's a rewarding challenge to tackle. But here's a word to the wise. Many churches have read about or visited these enhanced environments and then charged into the project without a full grasp of essentials such as wiring, ventilation, building codes or traffic flow, to name a few.

Creativity and enthusiasm are not the only prerequisites. If you're undertaking a sizeable redesign, you need professional expertise. Considering the amount of time and money you're going to invest in this venture and how many years it's going to be in place, it's a wise idea to bring in a professional interior designer to check the workability of your plan and suggest practical improvements. Professionals can save you unnecessary expenditures and frustration, and help you make good choices in areas such as materials, colors, furnishing, lighting, ventilation and space flow. An interior designer specializing in church school design brings a level of expertise to your project that you won't find in the volunteer pool of your congregation.

Fresh Eyes

It is hard to be objective about your own space. Fresh eyes see things you may be overlooking. Trained eyes see possibilities where you are unaware there are any. It's like working a jigsaw puzzle with all the pieces jumbled in front of you. A designer is able to imagine what the final picture will look like. A good designer will bring a clear sense of color, proportion and line to the design and will be able to visualize what rooms will look like with furniture and know whether removing a wall or adding a built-in will improve the space. Because all of these skills are applied to the whole project, the designer is able to establish a sense of continuity. By mixing different elements and establishing links between fabric, color, style and motif, designers help you create a satisfying space that is unified and functional rather than a series of separate rooms.

Experienced church school designers offer invaluable insights into multidimensional learning, Bible stories and themes and the process it takes to bring about a kid-friendly environment. They know the proper sequence for decisions about city codes, lighting, plumbing, wiring, fabrics, and furniture, and can help to avoid unnecessary expenditures by making sure that needs are met and the possibility of error is lessened. Their knowledge of scale and proportion assures that you'll purchase items that fit appropriately into your space.

Professional designers have access to a greater range of resources than the average consumer. They understand what kinds of fabrics stand up to hard use and comply with fire safety codes. The motifs and patterns in fabrics available to "the trade only" are extensive and, in most cases, can't be duplicated at the local fabric stores. Furnishings for these enriched environments are innovative. It's the designer's job to keep abreast of the latest products and trends and to think creatively about how to use them. Designers will design a piece they need and have it built if they are unable to find just the right "ready-made" item. It is also the designer's job to know about safety issues, water lines, electrical circuitry and building codes. This knowledge can help avoid costly mistakes or omissions.

There's No Substitute for Experience

Professionals who have designed dozens of church school spaces have learned to anticipate needs and avoid potential pitfalls. Investing in professional advice up front will save you headaches in the long run and ensure that you end up with a space that's both functional and beautiful.

A designer can coordinate with architects and contractors, detecting and solving problems before they're set in stone. It's easier to use an eraser than a sledge hammer! If you are remodeling your children's ministry area, the right designer will give you great insights into how to provide the most effective learning environment. If you are just now bringing this concept to your church board, a professional can be a great advocate to your pastor, various committees and your congregation by introducing concepts visually and verbally.

> Take your time in the **planning stage** and do it right! The care you take up front will mean saving time, money and frustration down the road.

Take your time in the planning stage and do it right! The care you take up front will mean saving time, money and frustration down the road.

Chapter Four
Planning Your New Design

"If you don't know where you're going, any road will get you there."

-Lewis Carroll, Alice in Wonderland

You've gained valuable insights on the "whys" of enriched learning environments and you know how to inspire God-given creativity in your team. Now you're ready to begin work on your new children's ministry area. Your first tool is not a hammer or paint brush—it's a pencil!

Your project involves church-owned space, a budget and a crew of volunteers who are bound to have differing opinions. So the first order of business is to write a strategic plan that sets you up for success.

Got Information?

Your first big step is to throw a party to gather information and create your strategic plan. Invite your children's ministry committee and anyone else who might be a valuable resource to a "Wrack Your Brain Party" complete with chocolate fondue, games and prizes that will get them pumped for the project.

Here's a simple party plan that will get you off and rolling.

Wrack Your Brain Party

- ☐ Send invitations via email. In the title line write, "Got Brains?" In the body of the email write, "We need them! Come take a dip in scrumptious chocolate fondue. We will mix fun, prizes and inspiration and hatch a plan for a fantastic new children's ministry area. See you at (time, place).

- ☐ Ask several people to bring "dippers" for your fondue. Include strawberries, cubed pound cake, mandarin oranges, fresh pineapple, marshmallows, pretzels, and shortbread cookies.

- ☐ For prizes, purchase brainstorming supplies: inexpensive sketch pads, pencils and pads of colorful sticky notes.

- ☐ At a party store, purchase "dealy-bob" headbands with sparkly balls or pinwheels that stick up on springs. You'll use these as thinking caps to get everyone in a creative state of mind.

- ☐ Make this simple but irresistible chocolate fondue in a slow cooker.
    - 12 ounces semisweet chocolate
    - 1/2 cup half-and-half
    - 1 to 3 tablespoons flavoring of your choice

- ☐ As guests arrive, have them earn their dealy-bob headbands by creating a tongue twister that includes their first or last name. For example: *Jan surely shares silly shells. Marty smashes Shirley's sassy sashes.* Have everyone find a partner. Partners say each other's tongue twisters five times fast, then award each other dealy-bobs.

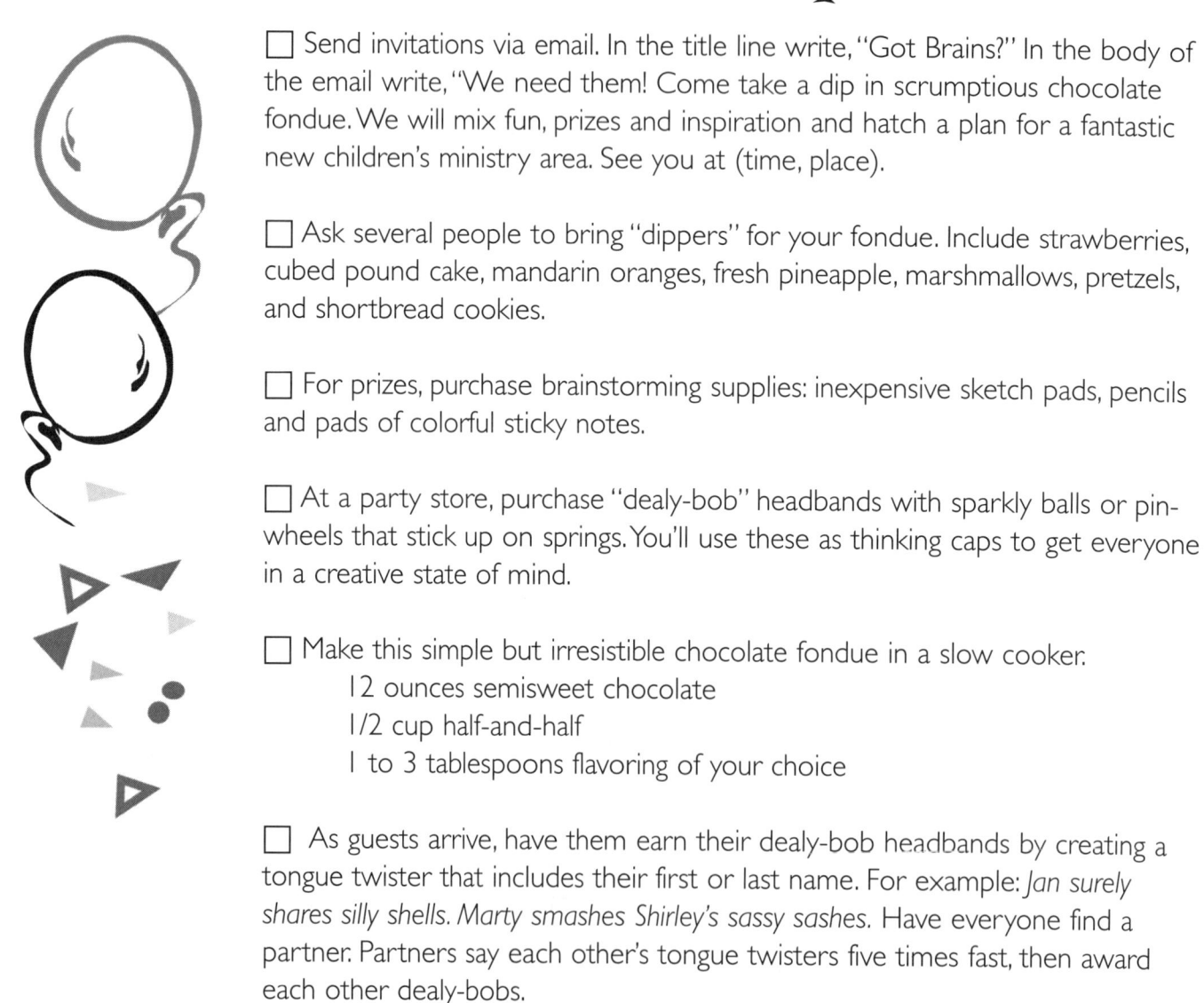

Great Spaces—Learning Places

☐ Dive into the fondue.

☐ Ask everyone to finish the sentence, "I'd like our children's ministry to be..." When they've finished the thought, let them pick planning supplies from the prize pile.

☐ Now that those brains are warmed up and humming, you're on to business.

Party Business

The business end of the "Wrack Your Brain" party involves gathering information and brainstorming.

Here's the information you need to gather:

1. What spaces in your church can be appropriated for children's ministry? Obtain blueprints and floor plans of your facility. Confirm with the appropriate committee which areas you can use for your children's program. Consider if these spaces are to be dedicated to Sunday morning use (permanent dedicated space) or if they are multiple use spaces, shared spaces with weekday programs, or flexible spaces. Then, go back through your whole facility again and look at it with fresh eyes. Could some rearranging be done to make a better accommodation for your plan? Is there a little nook or cranny you haven't considered? Any additional space you could use?

2. What were your Sunday school attendance numbers for the last 12 months and what is your projected growth for the next 12? Many churches experience attendance jumps of 20% or more in the first four months of opening their re-designed Sunday school. Experiential learning is activity based and requires different kinds of spaces. Plan on a maximum of 10-15 kids per workshop room. A room that is 375-400 square feet can handle this size class well.

3. What is a reasonable target date for completion of your project? Attached is a flow chart showing the development steps and the approximate time to allow for each stage. *Preparation is an important part in the development. Don't skimp on preparation time.* This is when you develop your Design Team and put dates on the calendar to realize your goals. Preparing your congregation for this exciting new change is a critical step. You'll need time to present your vision, manage their feelings and work out the details.

Planning Your New Design

Project Time-Line	
Programming	3 weeks
Concept Development	3 weeks
Design Development	10 weeks
Implementation	12-16 weeks
Observation/Celebration	3 weeks

4. What is your budget for implementing the design? How much will it cost? How much will be donated? How much will come from a building campaign? How much will come from the buildings and grounds budget? Any money coming from designated giving? How much will you develop in stages?

Remember the old joke about the auto repair shop that told clients that work could be done GOOD, FAST and CHEAP but they could only have two out of three? The same principle applies to design work. You can have it good and fast, but that's not cheap. You can have it good and cheap, but that's not going to be done quickly. And you can have it fast and cheap, but it won't be good! The key, then, is to plan enough time and enough money to result in a good job that will reap benefits for years to come.

On to the Plan

The information you've gathered provides the groundwork for your future decisions. Now you're ready to write a strategic plan to help you achieve your desired result. You'll needs lists, calendars and spreadsheets. A laptop computer or two with calendar programs would be a great help.

At this point be sure to include your senior pastor as well as any associate pastors and staff members who are connected to children's ministries.

It is vitally important that the senior pastor support your efforts and that other staff members are aware of and on board with the plans as well.

Your children's ministry committee would certainly be part of this group, along with any "centers of influence" (i.e., chairperson of Buildings & Grounds Committee, Properties Committee, Finance Committee). After one or two creative warm-ups from Chapter 3, begin your working time together by creating a mission statement. This statement will be the north star that will guide many future decisions.

Your Strategic Plan

1. Write your mission statement.

2. Write a situation and trend analysis.

3. Set goals and objectives.
   - Cast the vision.
   - Develop teams.
     - Curriculum Team
     - Teacher Team
     - Marketing Team
     - Building Team

     (Team leaders make up the Design Team)

4. Develop your work plan.

   All teams develop:
   - calendar
   - lists
   - budget

5. Market your ideas.

6. Celebrate and evaluate.

Planning Your New Design

Step 1: Develop a Mission Statement

Your mission statement may be an augmentation of your current children's ministries mission statement or a more child-focused version of your church's missions statement. Put in writing what your vision is. Make it clear and concise, memorable and meaningful, and be sure it coincides with your church mission statement. Include who, what, when and how. Here's an example:

> "To develop an experiential learning environment at XYZ Church to equip, inspire and train the first through sixth grade children in the Christian faith, beginning September 18, 2005."

This statement includes your vision (equip, inspire, train), the who (first through sixth graders), what (experiential learning environment), when (September 18th) and the how (develop it!).

Another example would be,

> "To implement multidimensional learning for Sunday school classes for first through sixth grade at XYZ Church, beginning September 18, 2005. To encourage the children to experience Biblical truths and faith stories so they may know and experience God, and lead them to owned faith."

In your project notebook, write "STRATEGIC PLAN" on the top of the page. Roman Numeral I is "Mission Statement." Write this as a team so everyone will buy into it and take ownership of it. People work harder and enjoy the process more if they are working to fulfill a shared dream.

Step 2: Situation and Trend Analysis

A Situation and Trend Analysis gets at the questions,
- What's going on at your church?
- What's going on in other churches and in the world that makes you want to plan for something new?

The issues discussed in Chapter One make up a key part of your situation analysis. You want to attract children to the church and help them learn and retain spiritual truths. Multidimensional learning produces higher levels of retention. The cultural situations we discussed were sporadic attendance and the affect of stress in children's lives.

The overload of the "information era" and the impact of constant video, internet and TV use leaves children over stimulated. Over-programmed lives leave little time for spiritual matters. The Search Institute Study (Minneapolis, 1990) is an excellent source for research on the directions main line denominations are moving and why working with children in an experiential way is vital to developing integrated faith. This study suggests that only a minority of adults have integrated faith. We need to change that! For up-to-date information contact Search Institute, 122 West Franklin Avenue, Suite 525, Minneapolis, MN 55404.

Step 3: S.W.O.T.

Finally, do a S.W.O.T. Inventory for your congregation. List your congregation's

- **Strengths**
- **Weaknesses**
- **Opportunities**
- **Threats** to success

in regard to developing this new kind of Sunday school.

Facilitate a brainstorming session for these four considerations, listing the input from your group on newsprint. This exercise helps you to be aware of issues you need to address, problems that need to be solved, and communication that needs to happen within your unique situation as you go about this process.

- Build on your strengths (i.e., involved congregation=lots of volunteers).

- Take action to bolster the weaknesses (i.e., no money budgeted).

- Advertise the opportunities you will have as a result of this new program (i.e., evangelism to children).

- Be watchful for threats against the project's success (i.e., lack of organization skills to coordinate volunteers).

All these considerations will feed into the step-by-step process of your strategic plan in the "objectives" portion which follows.

Step 4: Goals and Objectives

A goal is a statement written down to give you direction. (NOTE: The key to an effective strategic plan is that it is put in writing!) Goals usually begin with the word "To" followed by a verb. Your goals might look like this.

Goal 1: To cast the vision

Goal 2: To form the sub-committees

Goal 3: To select curriculum and space

Goal 4: To conduct training sessions

Goal 5: To implement the physical design

Goal 6: To thank volunteers and celebrate the project when it is finished.

Objectives are the steps you take to achieve your goal. Objectives are "SMART."

- **S**pecific
- **M**easurable
- **A**ffordable
- **R**ealistic
- **T**ime-directed

Some examples of objectives are:

Goal 1, Objective 1: Christian Educator and design consultant to meet with the Children's Committee, pastors and staff on February 23, 2005.

Goal 1, Objective 2: Pastor to introduce vision to congregation on March 13, 2005.

Be sure each of the objectives you write meets the SMART criteria. From your list of goals and objectives, you will be able to plug dates into the calendar for all upcoming meetings and deadlines. This will ensure that no step is forgotten. Your calendar is your best friend in organizing this plan. The easiest way, I find, is to use a computer calendar program.

The Work Plan in Detail

The detailed work plan allows you to achieve your life-long aspiration to be The King or Queen of Lists! And so, Your Highness, the resources you need to list include:

- People
- Money
- Donations
- Time lines

The calendar, as we mentioned above, is especially important during the implementation phase. Keep a master calendar with all activities listed on it. Include team meetings, ordering deadlines, delivery times and group work days. You may choose to be the Keeper of the Calendar yourself. Or, someone in your group who has great skill with spreadsheets may become the master organizer.

Polish Off the Lists

1) Put all objectives, tasks, meetings, and activities on the calendar for all committees.

2) Construct your budget

3) Assemble these team member lists for the following:

- Building Construction Team
- Curriculum Team
- Marketing Team
- Teacher Team

(The team leaders, along with Director of Children's Education will form your

Design Team and report weekly on progress in each area.)

Now that you have a calendar and lists in hand, you're ready to cast your vision to the congregation with the use of a well-prepared marketing plan.

Step 5: Marketing Plan 101

Know your "target market" here. Parents? Teachers? Children? Donors? Opposition? Yes to all, probably. Go back to your S.W.O.T. Inventory and pick up target market ideas from there. Know your market. Plan how you will reach them.

Marketing is how you cast the vision for this new children's ministry project to the congregation. This gets the adults and children alike excited about what is to come, helps them to buy into the concept, take ownership, volunteer and attend. Vision casting is carried on throughout the entire implementation of the design project. It begins as introducing the vision. From there the marketing team develops a plan to educate, communicate and motivate the congregation.

Four areas you want to consider in your marketing plan are:

1. Introducing your new Sunday school.
   - Plan an introductory meeting for your church.
   - Create brochures.
   - Consider building a web site and bringing in someone from another church who can share the success of this approach to children's ministry.

2. Explaining why enriched environments are important to teaching your children.
   - Bring in experts to cast the vision. Besides the information given earlier chapters, you'll find help on the following websites:
     www.churchschooldesign.com
     www.childrensministries.org
     www.sundaysoftware.com
   - Consider planning a seminar where adults can attend and experience "workshops" for themselves.

3. Open Communication Lines
Create a climate of acceptance and communicate your vision. You and your committee might wear buttons that say "Ask Me About A NEW KIND OF SUNDAY SCHOOL" and wear them on Sunday morning. Speak one-on-one about the wonderful opportunities that will come from this new design plan. Remember to listen to concerns—dialog with people. Take their suggestions and thank them.

4. Consider marketing the idea of enriched environment learning through:
- publicity to the kids
- fact sheets about the project in the narthex
- staff meeting
- bulletin insert
- Power Point presentations
- brochures
- videos
- church newsletter (a column for "A New Kind of Sunday School")

Planning Your New Design

Once you've chosen your marketing strategies, your strategic plan is complete. Congratulations! Your next—and very important!—step is to present your strategic plan to your church's governing board for approval. Review the plan with your senior pastor and discuss the optimum timing for your presentation. This is your opportunity to cast the vision and gain the enthusiastic endorsement of the broader base of church leadership.

When the Light Turns Green

You can approach the job ahead with confidence because you've done a thorough job of laying the groundwork. And, most importantly, your work will culminate in giving the children in your church incredible opportunities to learn who God is and to respond to his love.

Use your strategic plan as your coach for the mission ahead. Keep your eye on the goal. Print calendars with important dates for everyone on the team. Set a weekly update time for key players. Do it by email when you need to. Enlist a prayer and encouragement team. And, enjoy the journey!

The Theme's the Thing

The theme you choose for your new children's area plays an incredibly important role in marketing your ministry for years to come. Our society responds to logos and images: golden arches, the swish, one large and two smaller intersecting circles that make a certain mouse, and a creamy white mustache, to name a few. As you ponder your choice of theme, what simple, intriguing images come to mind? What short, catchy phrase puts your purpose in a nutshell and ties your varied workshops together? This is important stuff! What will pique kids' interest, imply your purpose and lend itself to strong visual expression? Cruise through several workshop rotation/multidimensional learning websites (just enter those topics in a search engine) and see what other churches have done. What themes appeal to you? Why?

My advice for starting your design work is to begin with a focal point. You need to have a direction to take your design ideas and a central focus that helps it hang together. The easiest way to do this is to create a name for your new kind of Sunday school (i.e., "The Kingdom"), then give a theme to each of the classrooms. Theming the rooms gives focus to your design and adds immeasurable interest for the children and adults alike.

Theming gets our attention. The physical space is precisely and creatively designed to keep our minds focused on the reason that brought us there. And it's effective, so long as it's done well.

Creating a verbal picture of what you are envisioning for your church must be done early in your design process to create unity in your design. Call your committee together to brainstorm ideas of how you want your space to look. What's the overall theme, feel, design you want to achieve? Do you want an "old world" look or a more updated look? Are you working off of a keyword in a mission statement (i.e., *journey* or *caring*)?

Remember to start your brainstorming with a creativity warm-up from Chapter 3. Next, make an introductory statement about your new kind of Sunday school. Read your mission statement out loud. Then ask your team to say whatever the statement brings to mind. "Dumb" ideas are welcome!

Combined with other input they can become brilliant. Censor nothing. Don't allow participants to use "stoppers" that criticize and bring the brainstorming to a halt. You'll have plenty of time to narrow down your list as the process continues.

When you're brainstorming, sticky notes are your friends! They can be prioritized, shuffled, and put together in pleasing combinations. It's not a big risk to put up a little sticky note. This tactic helps to get every idea up on the wall.

Honing In

Once you get some pleasing word combinations, you can make connections. Group related words and phrases together. Have everyone anonymously list their top three or four selections. You'll be surprised at how quickly consensus develops. Take your top choices and develop them a bit. For instance, "Journey Land would look like… and would include…" Write down all ideas on newsprint and tape them around the room.

Save your final decision for another meeting. In the meantime, encourage helpers to come back with theme-related workshop ideas and decorating schemes. It will soon become apparent which choices provide a fruitful starting point for further development. By your second meeting, it's very likely that the "right" theme will resonate with nearly everyone.

Now you have a plan and a cornerstone on which to build. On to the details. The fun begins!

Chapter Five

Design Development—It's All in the Details

"Art is a collaboration between God and the artist, and the less the artist does the better."
- Andre Gide

Are you ever going to have fun with this part of the process! You've done the planning, gotten approval and come up with a compelling theme for your children's ministry area. Now you're ready to dig into the design itself, with the colors of the rainbow as your palette and your God-given creativity as your guide. This is one of those rare times when, as an adult, you get to feel like a kid in a toy shop!

We'll walk through the principles of good design, then send you on a hunt to find just the right colors, fabrics and accessories to create a one-of-kind Bible learning zone for the children in your ministry.

Principles and Elements of Design

Take a deep breath—here comes your crash course in design. Think of these key design principles as the signposts that will guide you along the road to success.

You've probably experienced plenty of bad design in your life. Did you ever stay in a motel room that you just couldn't wait to leave? Or attend a meeting where the buzz of the lights, uncomfortable chairs and noise from next door made it next to impossible to accomplish a thing? Poor design is more than offensive to the eye—it hampers productivity. Lack of harmony causes people to feel distracted and uneasy. Poor proportion makes us feel off-balance. Inappropriate color choices can cause everything from irritation to drowsiness. And clutter is a real focus killer. Let's tackle these issues so your new learning place will welcome, inspire and bring focus.

Elements of Design (objects)

> Design elements are the things you have to work with.

SPACE
How large is the room? Is it enclosed or open? How is it shaped?

FORM
Are the walls, doorways and ceilings rectangular, triangular or circular? What is the room's dominant form?

LINE
Is the direction dominantly vertical or horizontal? Are there many directions that cause confusion? Any structural patterns in the room? Arches? Raised panel doors? Columns? Or a lack thereof? Play up the architectural interest you have. If you're working in a ho-hum square box, add "faux" details for interest.

TEXTURE
Do you have a pleasing variety of rough, smooth, plain and complex surfaces? Vary the textures. If you have brick walls, introduce variety with smooth surfaces such as laminated counter tops, grained woods and soft fabrics.

COLOR
What "must keep" colors do you have in the brick, wood or flooring? Avoid primary colors (red, yellow, blue) which scream for attention. Use complex, sophisticated colors for stress relief and interest.

ORNAMENTATION/PATTERN
What structural patterns are in the room? Can you add to them or play off them? An arched window can be revisited in the arched back of a chair. Accessorizing the room is fun and important, but resist! It is the last thing you do. Be strong and curb your impulse to buy accessories until you know exactly what the room needs.

Principles of Design (what you do with objects)

> Design principles guide what you do with those things.

BALANCE
Build balanced rooms. Divide the room in quarters and be sure each quarter has the same amount of "visual weight." Distribute furniture in a balanced way in all quadrants of the room. If all the big furniture must be at one end of the room, hang a large mural on the opposite wall to offset it.

RHYTHM
Create rhythm to carry the eye around the room by repeating a color three times or more. Or, repeat shapes around the room. Evenly distribute the lighting, then use accents to bring out a pleasing repetition.

EMPHASIS
Find a focal point that will immediately draw the eye. Play it up. Build off of it. Don't allow equally dominant spaces to compete with it.

HARMONY
Produce harmony by balancing variety and unity. You need both to bring the room together. Avoid a hodge-podge look by seeing the room as a whole. Select a variety of textures, colors, styles of furnishings and purposely place these items. And, stick to your color scheme, right down to the waste paper baskets!

SCALE/PROPORTION
How do the sizes of various elements in the room look in proportion to each other? Is the signage in good proportion to the door or hallway it's used in? Is the lettering big enough to see? Are your "faux" pillars big enough for a room with a vaulted ceiling? Is the mural on the wall in scale with the size of the wall? Avoid the common mistake of creating clutter by using too many small things.

- Create a space that looks inviting and balanced and works well for the activities it will host.
- Avoid a cluttered, distracting, hodge-podge look.

Design Development—It's All in the Details

ONE MORE BIGGIE
- **STORAGE, Storage, Storage!**

If materials are not essential to the lesson of the day, store them behind closed doors so they won't distract young learners.

Tackling the Workshop Rooms

There's your crash course! Now you're ready to set up a Classroom Specifications Worksheet for each room.

Photocopy a separate worksheet for each room. List the verbal picture you have come up with in your Design Concept writing and then list everything you will need in that room. Consider the shell of the room, (floor, walls, ceiling, windows, stairways, fireplaces). Then list all the furniture, finishes, equipment and accessories.

Mount your worksheets in a large binder. Use a tabbed divider for each room. Add sketches, fabric samples and photos from catalogs behind the worksheet. Now for a step-by-step walk through each item on the worksheet.

Classroom Specifications Worksheet

Workshop name:

Workshop description:

Signage:

Floor plan: (see attached)

Walls: (see elevations and fabric samples)

Furnishings: (see furniture selection sheets and fabric samples)

Window treatments:

Flooring: (see carpet and tile samples)

Ceiling/Lighting: (see lighting plan)

Equipment:

Accessories: (see selection sheet)

Permission to photocopy this page granted for local church use. Copyright © Cook Communications Ministries. Printed in *Great Spaces, Learning Places* by Jan Hubbard.

Workshop Name and Description

Choosing your theme, your workshops and their names was part of your strategic planning. Each workshop will carefully and cleverly carry the theme forward, while creating its own distinct character and purpose. Check out http://www.rotation.org/whatcall.php, a web site where rotation churches share their workshop names and themes.

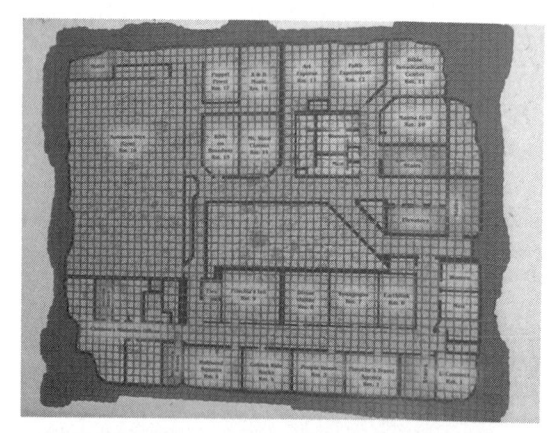

Signage

When parents and kids approach a multidimensional learning area, they need to know who goes where. Particularly in the workshop rotation model, clear signage is extremely important. It's your first opportunity to show that this learning model is user friendly. While signs need to be attractive, their primary purpose is to show the way.

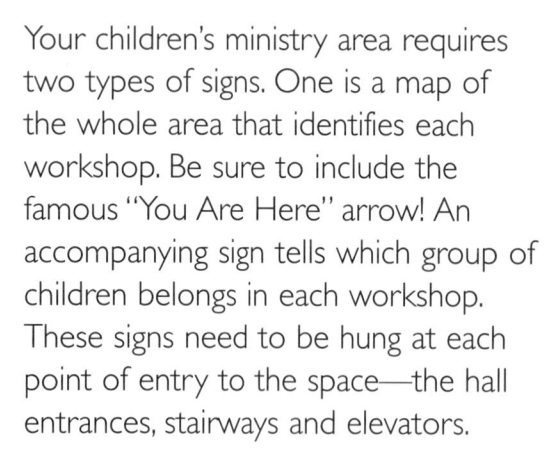

Your children's ministry area requires two types of signs. One is a map of the whole area that identifies each workshop. Be sure to include the famous "You Are Here" arrow! An accompanying sign tells which group of children belongs in each workshop. These signs need to be hung at each point of entry to the space—the hall entrances, stairways and elevators.

A second type of sign identifies each room or workshop. Make sure they're large enough to be seen clearly.

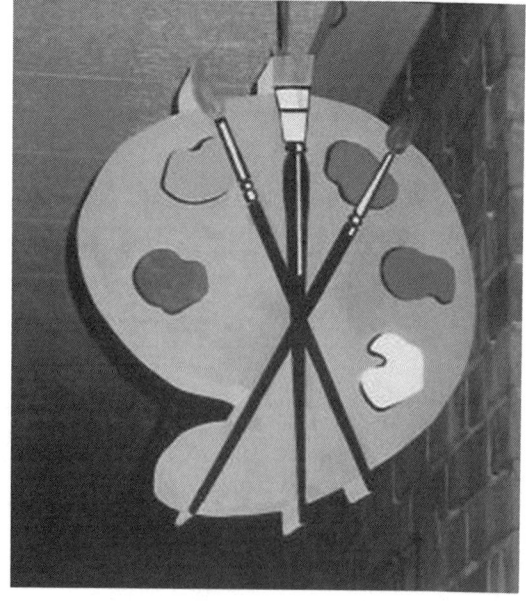

page 58   Great Spaces—Learning Places

Floor Plan

Lay out your room on grid paper (1/4" = 1 foot). Draw door swings, built-ins and changes in flooring (i.e., where carpet changes to tile). When you sketch your floor plan, use an angelic perspective, as if you're hovering on the ceiling and looking down on the tops of all the surfaces in the room.

A floor plan includes anything that touches the floor. The exception is windows. Put an open space within your wall line to represent the placement of the windows. Draw upper cabinets with a dotted line. Next, measure the furniture you are using and draw it in the space. Be sure you have two feet of space to pull chairs out from tables. You'll need approximately three feet for traffic patterns in the room and open space for activities.

Floor Plan
- [ ] use grid paper
- [ ] 1/4" = 1 foot
- [ ] include everything that touches the floor
- [ ] include window and door openings, architectural features
- [ ] allow two feet for chair movement around tables
- [ ] allow three feet for traffic flow

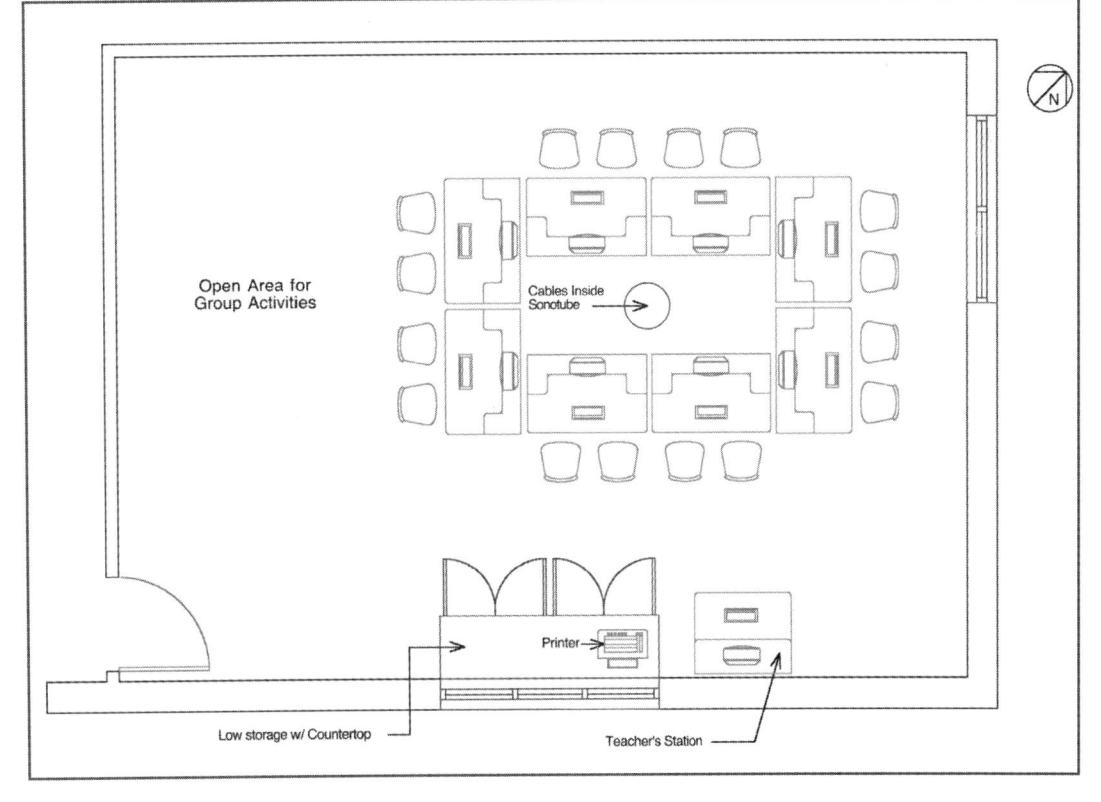

A simple and inexpensive way to add architectural interest to a room is by adding faux columns. Include such features in your floor plan, as well as built-in loft areas and raised platform seating.

If your strategic plan includes a computer room, ask the computer expert who is

Design Development—It's All in the Details

overseeing the program if there is a preferred placement for the computers. Two popular layouts are the perimeter style and center circle style. The perimeter style simply lines up the computers around the walls of the room, leaving the center of the room open. The circular style is a more interactive setup with computers facing each other around an enclosed center table configuration. This layout allows for a more creative design scheme but does require more space.

Lofts and Little Places

A small loft adds great interest to any room. Children love to sit up above and down below in these cozy areas. They fit the décor of an old Israeli household. They can also provide a comfy reading nook or a contemporary hangout for older children. They only need to be three feet high with a two-foot railing.

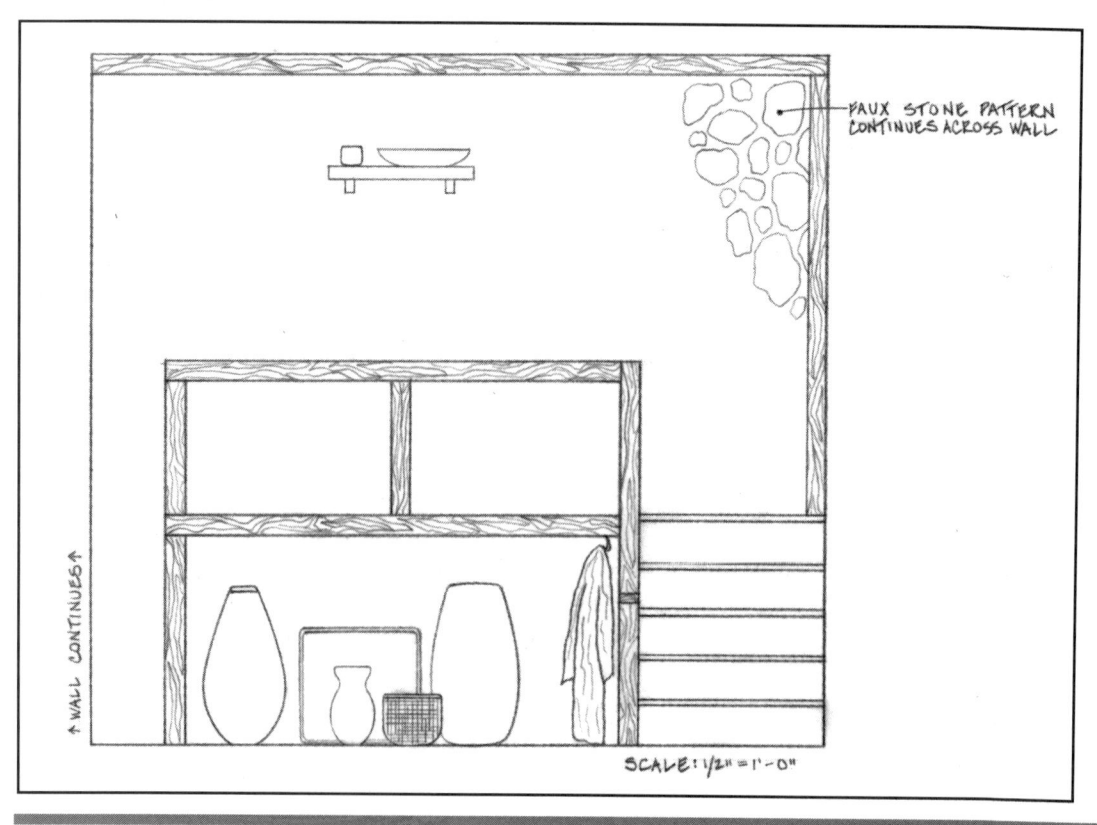

Great Spaces—Learning Places

Storage

How much storage is enough? Most churches believe that more is always better, but we are finding that with experiential learning, we use fewer supply "staples" that used to be needed in each room. Your storage needs will be determined by your overall room assignments. If you are designing age-level rooms (separate, permanent space for each grade level, for example) you will need to plan for a diversity of activity in each room. Traditionally we think in terms of cabinetry. If you are adding cabinetry, you will need to select from wood, laminate, and painted finishes. Millwork is expensive, however, and there are alternatives that are effective as well as fun and innovative.

Different workshops call for different kinds of storage. Art workshops, for instance, need regular cabinetry with doors that close. Label the doors A, B, C, etc. Beneath the cabinets, hang a laminated sheet that details what's in cabinet A, cabinet B and so on.

Open bookshelves provide inexpensive storage, but they get disorganized easily and present a cluttered appearance. Solve this dilemma by using storage baskets on the shelves. Canvas-lined baskets can be removed as the contents are needed, then put back neatly. Stackable wooden crates work wonderfully for puppets and other kinds of storage, and they can be painted to complement the room.

My firm has prepared a neat little design for simple cabinets that have hooks for coats on one side and a drama wall canvas on the other. The canvas can be changed for other workshops. This kind of double-duty unit is invaluable. It keeps clutter out of sight and continues the theme of the room.

Moveable storage items I've created include an art pyramid on wheels, a market cart that holds supplies for any kind of workshop, yet fits in beautifully with Bible-time themes, and a portable drama wall with canvas on one side and hooks for costumes on the other. To order plans for these units, see page 109.

Walls and Color

Wall treatments give you endless possibilities for enhancing your environment. Paint stretches your dollars further than any other medium. Subtle or dramatic, great color can redefine and update a room. You can select the color you think you want from those little paint chips at the paint store, but the best way to determine if the color is what you want is to purchase a quart of paint, brush it out on the wall, and let it dry. Light affects how the color looks. You may have happily or unhappily discovered that principle in your home painting projects. Your best bet is to try the color on the wall.

Let's talk about color.

The use of primary colors for children was introduced in the last century when it was believed children needed extra stimulation. Because of the stress that permeates our society, children need a retreat, a place to calm down and relax. Now we choose more soothing colors. Cool colors calm, but that doesn't mean we need to restrict the palette to blues, greens and violets. We can choose from the warm side of the pallet also—reds, oranges—yellows, but use toned down colors. As an example, the hue (or color) you select may be in the orange family, but a wise choice would be a brick or a terra cotta. These toned down colors are more calming than a pure, intense orange. Muted colors from the orange family blend well with khaki green or soft violet blue. For grades K-6, juxtapose warm, bright color schemes with cool colors as an accent. This balance reduces tension and anxiety.

Undertones are also something you need to watch. Have you heard the term "church beige"? Many of us are inundated with that color in our buildings. And there are probably 52 shades of beige—each with a different undertone! Some have a rose undertone, some have a green undertone, and so on. The key is to avoid mixing undertones that are not compatible.

Choosing colors is one of the most difficult tasks for an untrained eye. I have a friend who recently built a new house. She painted a bedroom and bath three times before she was satisfied with the result. Professional help is invaluable at this point, unless you have a real fondness for painting!

I usually select the fabrics for a room first, then coordinate the paint colors with that fabric. The fabric automatically selects your color scheme for you. If you like the blend of colors in the fabric, you'll probably like it in the rest of the room as well.

The lowly baseboard is the foundation of your wall treatment. If you are able to replace the baseboard (most classrooms have a vinyl base), select a color that blends with your walls and flooring.

Divide and Conquer

In multiple use spaces, you may need to use paneled dividers. There is a wide range of product available to meet your needs: operable partitions (movable, suspended from tracks), self-support systems, portable panels, accordion partitions and mobile partitions. Acoustics in partition walls are not as effective as in a structural wall, but they have improved a great deal over the years. You can purchase special acoustical panels that are designed for noise reduction. Some of these partitions have tackable faces, some can be painted, and some are made of glass. I have found a good variety at Hufcor (www.hufcor.com), a manufacturer of partitions and operable walls.

With shared spaces, it's a good idea to use portable furniture that can be stored outside of the room and brought in on an as-needed basis. Our firm has designed portable art storage, drama "walls" with storage, game boards and "market carts" that can hold a variety of activities. While these items require their own storage area, they will free up much needed classroom floor space. Lap top computers can be stored on a cart and go from room to room as needed (provided each room is wired or you have wireless).

Design Development—It's All in the Details

In the Appendix you'll find a plan for a built-in cabinet that works beautifully for shared spaces. Alternating arrangements of the cabinet doors allow for access to two separate storage areas, with different décor exposed in each arrangement.

Furnishings

First, determine what existing furnishings you can use in the room and what you will need to purchase or build. On your floor plan, draw in the furniture to scale. As an example, you may decide to use tables with stools, rather than chairs, to give a creative, artsy feel to a room. Maybe you have selected stools that stack for storage and tables that can be moved to the perimeter of the room to make a large open activity area in the middle. You will need to measure and draw the floor plan both ways.

Also consider the scale of the furniture. For children, scaled down items are comforting and create a sense of security. This is one reason children respond well to sitting on pillows on the floor instead of chairs, climbing up onto a loft area or snuggling in a reading corner. These guidelines will help you choose appropriate furnishings.

Now you're ready to sketch an elevation or perspective of the wall or space. Don't be shy if your sketch is less than a masterpiece. Its purpose is to help everyone on your team visualize your ideas and implement them accurately.

Furnishings

- ☐ based on activity needs
- ☐ tables—high/low options
- ☐ seating—not just chairs
- ☐ based on theme of room
- ☐ ergonomically correct

Age	Seat Height	Table Height
Toddler	10" – 12"	18" – 20"
Pre K-K	12" – 14"	20" – 22"
Grades 1-5	14" – 16"	22" – 26"
Grades 6 & up	16" – 18"	26" – 29"

Window Treatments

How much space is there in the window frame? Enough to mount blinds or shades in the inside of the frame (approximately three inches), or will they need to be mounted outside the frame? Note the distance from window to floor and window to ceiling. Check for any heat registers below the window. If there are heating elements near the window, you must design treatments that don't touch those elements.

Considering the window type, size and placement, begin your creative solutions. First, consider the direction the window faces. Do you need light and temperature control? Under-treatments such as blinds and light-blocking film will solve your light control needs. A variety of thermal treatments can allow light as they block heat and cold. An excellent resource for window solutions is *The Encyclopedia of Window Fashions* by Charles T. Randall (1997, Randall International, Orange, CA). This book illustrates hundreds of window treatment options along with yardage charts and measuring information.

Design Development—It's All in the Details

Windows
- ❏ fabric?
- ❏ blinds?
- ❏ faux stained glass?
- ❏ light control?
- ❏ temperature control?

In keeping with our "No Clutter" criteria, plan clean, simple window treatments that make a statement in the room. Often the best choice is blinds with a top treatment. You'll need full draperies in special cases such as a drama stage, but generally a minimal treatment brings softness and simple motifs into the design of the room, coordinating space with shape and fabric.

Flat panels show the fabric pattern the best, so if your fabric is the core of your design for the room, do a flat valance. You can make the bottom edge interesting—diamond shaped points, fringe, trim. Also, hanging the valance from the ceiling line uses a larger amount of fabric, thereby showing off the pattern better.

Make a rainbow for your window by putting a sleeve of multicolored fabric around dryer venting. The crinkle effect of the tubing will gather the fabric into an interesting pattern. Then mount the dryer venting at the top of the window using fishing line and cup hooks, hanging it in a rainbow shape.

Great Spaces—Learning Places

About Fabrics

Look for fabrics that are age appropriate and durable. You'll find a wonderful selection of fabrics for nurseries, toddlers and young children but it's a bit more difficult to find the right fabric for elementary ages. Be consistent with the theme of the room. You wouldn't put a Laura Ashley™ floral in a Bible-time room—chintzes didn't exist in 30 AD! Coarsely woven fabrics in stripes and earth tones work for that time period. Contemporary prints (which the kids love!) work well for rooms with modern themes.

Fabrics come in various weights. Don't upholster with drapery weight fabric. But you may want to experiment with a drapery treatment that is made from upholstery weight fabric. Some top treatments, such as cornices and flat valances, work well in heavy fabric.

Fabrics
- ☐ flame-retardant
- ☐ colorful
- ☐ theme-based
- ☐ appropriate for kids

Focus on Flooring

The most-used floor coverings are paint, resilient flooring and woven soft floor coverings. Paint is the most inexpensive and offers great creative options, but is not a good choice for heavy traffic and usage areas. Resilient flooring (sheet goods or tiles) are a good choice for "messy use" areas such as arts, crafts, science and cooking rooms. Woven soft floor coverings are excellent for

Flooring
- ☐ tile?
- ☐ carpet?
- ☐ artificial turf?
- ☐ cushioned sports flooring?
- ☐ painted design?

less messy areas. They provide comfort, warmth and make the room inviting. Children spend time on the floor, especially in rooms with low seating such as bean bags and pillows. Use commercial grade carpet in classrooms. It's durable and easy to clean. Softer oriental-style throw rugs from a discount or home improvement store add rich, inviting color and texture. For large motor movement rooms, you may want to check into specialty cushioned flooring.

Equipment

Equipment needs follow the purpose of the rooms. Storytelling and art rooms can be "low tech." Newsrooms, computer labs, theaters and game rooms require fairly sophisticated electronics. If you are purchasing new equipment, due diligence is important. Find out what is new and state of the art, then adjust your expectations to your budget!

If you're setting up a computer lab, check out Neil McQueen's site, www.SundaySoftware.com for recommendations on hardware and software.

Equipment
- ☐ TV?
- ☐ VCR/DVD player?
- ☐ LCD projector?
- ☐ screen?
- ☐ speakers?
- ☐ CD player?
- ☐ camcorder?
- ☐ computers?
- ☐ Internet access?
- ☐ printers?
- ☐ electronic game boards?
- ☐ oven?
- ☐ bread machine?
- ☐ microwave?

Accessories

Interior designers are fond of saying, "Design is in the details." Coordinating your look with accessories is an important part of your room design. In every room you will need a clock and a wastebasket that coordinate with the color scheme and theme.

Typical "Bible time" accessories include:

- faux plants
- artifact reproductions
- faux fruits and vegetables
- baskets
- rugs
- pottery
- market carts
- striped awnings
- pillows

Remember that scale is important in accessorizing. Most people tend to go too small, so watch your selections. This is where we can get to the "clutter" look in a hurry.

Serrv, International is a non-profit, alternative trade and development organization that has a catalog of wonderful gifts from around the world. They have baskets, wall décor, rugs, and accessories that fit into many room themes.

Another good source for accessories for that old world look is *The Source for Everything Jewish*, a mail order catalog that is just that! Contact them at www.jewishsource.com.

"Design is in the details."

Now let's move on to a sampling of exciting specialty effects that will add warmth and wow factor to the walls and ceilings of your new children's ministry area.

Chapter Six

Fun Ways with Walls and Ceilings

"Then the LORD said to Moses, 'See I have chosen Bezalel... and I have filled him with the Spirit of God, with skill, ability and knowledge in all kinds of crafts—to make artistic designs for work in gold, silver and bronze to cut and set stones, to work in wood, and to engage in all kinds of craftsmanship... Also I have given skill to all the craftsmen to make everything I have commanded you."

-from Exodus 31:1-6

What can you do with a wall? Just about anything!

You can turn it into a desert, a market, a beach by the Sea of Galilee, a synagogue, a lush jungle, a star spangled sky, a library or a view from space. You can give it a window or even a whole row of windows that aren't really there. The view from the window can be of Bethlehem, the Jordan River, a vineyard or a city. You can make it of ancient, crumbling stone or turn it into a wall of water.

The wall is a palette. Wallpaper and paint are your tools, and in this case, the sky is not the limit! You can transform a wall for the price of paint.

Keep in mind that the walls are just one aspect of your overall design. A well-dressed wall will complement and finish the room, not serve as a distraction. But nothing can quite compare to the impact of a well-placed mural or trompe l'oeil ("fool the eye") feature.

Fun Ways with Walls and Ceilings   page 71

Choosing Paint

Not all paints are created equal. Many professional designers specify Benjamin Moore paint because its coverage, durability, and color quality is superior. Cheaper paints may be tempting, but they are a not a bargain in the long run. They will cover less square feet and often require more coats to get the same coverage as one coat of quality paint.

The finish options of paint include flat, eggshell, semi-gloss and high gloss. A semi-gloss is best for classrooms. It will tolerate some cleaning.

Tricks with Bricks

Brick walls present particular challenges. On a brick wall where you want to bring in some kid-friendly design but cannot paint, consider stretching fabric on large frames and hanging them by securing the screws in the grout area between the bricks. They can be removed and the grout repaired when needed. You may also paint murals on 4' x 8' pieces of wallboard and attach them to the walls in the same manner.

If you have permission to paint brick walls, a wonderful effect is to rag roll them. In one room we did, we painted a base coat of a creamy gold color (beware: the brick and grout soak up a lot of paint so use primer and be prepared for two applications of paint). Then rag roll a lighter shade of cream over the top. The result is a wonderful faux stone effect.

Fun Ways with Walls and Ceilings

Wallpaper Wonders

Wallpaper can carry off a theme for you, as well. In one church I named a classroom "Buried Treasure." Each Sunday the children searched scripture and maps there to find valuable biblical truths. The wallpaper was a Treasure Island theme. We selected our other colors in the room based on that wallpaper. The Internet is a fantastic place to peruse wallpaper patterns. You can find every kind of stone and brick work that look so real you have to touch them to tell for sure. Enter search words such as "wallpaper stone" into your web browser. You will come across sites that offer you wallpapers in stone patterns of every shape and color. Many will send samples for a small fee.

At home improvement stores and specialty wall covering stores you can browse through dozens of books of custom wallpapers. This may be an exercise you want to do with your design committee to find inspiration and make color choices. Your browsing for wallpapers may well influence the rest of your design choices for a given room. And remember, you don't need to wallpaper every wall for a pleasing result. One or two walls may be papered—others may be painted in coordinating colors.

Wallpaper can also be a wonderful choice for the hallways of your children's ministry area. A hand-hewn stone pattern brings a mellow, ancient warmth that works well with accessories such as wooden carts with artificial fruits and vegetables, pottery jars, striped awnings and baskets—both faux and real.

Great Spaces—Learning Places

When children enter this area, they literally step back into Bible times.

Wallpaper borders can carry out a theme and set the stage for the rest of the wall, with coordinating painted surfaces above and below. While you're looking at wallpaper, check into printed, pastable murals as well. You'll find archways, pillars, faux windows and sea scenes beautifully printed from professional artists' work.

Ceilings

As one of the largest solid surfaces of your room, the ceiling can add stunning impact to your design. Think of painting the ceiling to resemble a sky and adding birds or stars. "Trompe l'oeil" painting gives the illusion of being three dimensional. It is a French term that means "fool the eye." You may hang accents from the ceiling. Or, for a dramatic effect, hang flame retardant treated fabric from the ceiling or add beams to a room. Faux or real beams bring an old world look.

How to Go Faux

Faux finishes are a great effect for wallboard walls. They give a textured look, add warmth and interest, and disguise fingerprints and markings. It's also a "forgiving" look compared to flat paint. When you paint one color, especially when you select a higher sheen, any defect in the wall will become more prominent.

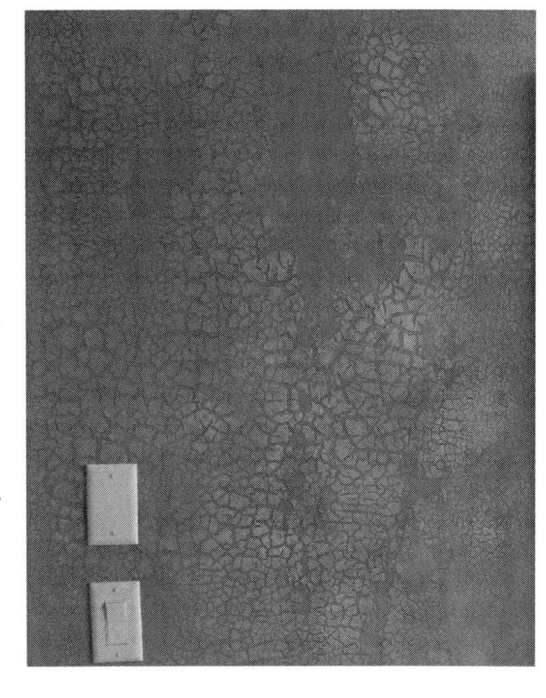

Fun Ways with Walls and Ceilings

Faux painting (faux is the French word for "false") may sound sophisticated and difficult—and some techniques are, to be honest. But you can achieve wonderful effects with just a bit of basic knowledge. A skilled painter can make a plain wall look like gleaming marble or ancient stonework.

Basic techniques can bring a very appealing aged feel. First-timers can achieve very satisfying results, bringing warmth and character to walls that would otherwise be plain and lacking in personality. WARNING: faux painting is fun, inexpensive, and with a little practice the results are spectacular. If you faux paint your workshop rooms, it's only fair to warn your spouse that your faux painting binge may continue at home!

Nearly every home improvement and paint store offers free demonstration classes in faux painting techniques. Most large paint manufacturers have displays of various effects and how to achieve them. To see an even wider sampling of ideas, type "faux painting" into your web browser and prepare to be amazed at the wealth of material that comes up on your screen. Your library will probably have several books on this ever-growing trend.

Try new techniques and color combinations on scrap surfaces. Once you're satisfied with the effect, start on an obscure wall—one that's behind a door, for instance. Painting a small area gives you a feel for the technique and lets you see if you're on track. If you need to make adjustments, swoosh on a little base coat and within fifteen minutes you'll be ready to have another go.

Faux painting can also be used as a corrective measure if your wall color turns out too strong. The color washing technique explained below can soften and tone down, or brighten and lighten—depending on the colors you choose. Even pros use faux to tweak their color schemes.

It's always good to faux with a friend. You'll work the wall in chunks, and in order to avoid a patchy look and hard edges, you need to move from one space to the next while the paint is still workable. Adding a faux finishing glaze to your paint keeps it "open" and workable for a longer period than you would have with paint straight from the can. When you tag team with a friend or two, you don't have to hurry. You can relax and enjoy the creative process and get a little paint in each other's hair.

So are you ready to have a go at faux? Let's walk through some simple faux techniques that result in striking settings for your rooms.

Colorwashing

This is one of the simplest faux painting techniques. It's a great solution if your original wall color isn't quite what you hoped. Mix faux glaze with a paint color in a 1:1 ratio. (For a very thin wash, you can stir in water until the mixture is creamy.) Using a sponge, an old brush or a wadded rag, apply the glaze to the wall in a circular washing motion. When the glaze has dried, you may add another glaze in the same color to deepen the wash if you wish.

Ancient Walls

Basecoat the wall with a warm beige color. Choose a medium gold for contrast. Mix the gold paint with faux glaze in a 1:1 proportion. Work with two or three people. One person rolls the darker color loosely onto the wall,

Fun Ways with Walls and Ceilings

leaving a few gaps here and there. Helpers with wadded cotton T shirts or cheesecloth press and smudge them into the wall, loosening and blending the color so the lighter basecoat shows through. Work in about three-foot sections. The glaze will keep your top coat workable for several minutes, but if you let it dry you'll be disappointed with hard edges that appear in your design.

The key to this technique is, once you start a wall, keep at it until you've finished. Roll on, rag off. For a more sophisticated effect, rag on a neutral gray here and there as the gold is drying. Just a touch, and maybe a few cracks and crumbles for character. Voilà—you've just aged a wall a millennium or two.

Sponging

This technique is as fun and simple as it gets. You base coat one color. While the base coat is still damp, dip a sponge into another color that is two shades lighter or two shades darker. Mix faux painting glaze into the contrasting paint and sponge it loosely on the wall. I often use this effect with shades of blue in multimedia rooms. Blue is a great background for human skin.

Different sponges give different effects, with natural sea sponges being the most textural. A large car-washing sponge is great, especially when you're covering

page 78   Great Spaces—Learning Places

long walls. You can achieve an open, playful look with sponging if you're careful not to overwork it. You'll need to step back from the wall every few minutes to gauge the effect. It's hard to judge what you're doing when you're just an arm's length from the wall.

There's a simple way to make this look more sophisticated. Set out two contrasting shades of paint that have been mixed with glaze. They need to be close in value so you don't get a messy, hodge-podge look. Dip one end of a large sponge into one color; dip the other end into the other color. Then sponge away. The second contrasting color might even have a bit of pearl or metal added for a bit of kick. Your friendly paint counter person can guide you to pearl and metallic products.

Stone Blocks

If you tackle old stone blocks, pin-striping tape will be your best friend. Lay out level pencil or chalk lines to mark the rows. Cover the rows securely with pin striping tape. When your painting is finished, you'll remove the tape and have instant "grout." Purchase a light warm beige, a medium warm beige, and a slightly darker gray-beige. Decorator displays in paint departments will guide you to the right trio of colors. Mix the paints with glaze in separate trays.

Use a wide decorator brush. Drag your brush across several stones. Without rinsing the brush, go into another color and drag it as well. Repeat with the third color. If you wish, use a dry, stiff brush to pounce and blend the colors.

> Decide where your light source will be.

Decide where your light source will be and use the darkest color on the edges of the stones away from the light. Use the lightest color to stroke a few highlights on the edge of the stone that would catch the light. Blend and pounce until you're happy with the effect. Then use an a old toothbrush to spatter paint some of each color onto the stone surface. Remove the tape and your ancient wall is set in stone!

You can purchase large stone stencils. Adhere them to the wall with spray-on stencil adhesive. Use your light, medium and dark stone colors on three separate sponges. Sponge, overlap and blend the colors. Removing the stencil reveals the grout lines.

Fun Ways with Walls and Ceilings

Sky

Skies are quick and fun. Basecoat with a muted blue that works well with the other colors in the room. (Don't go too bright or the sky will smack you in the face every time you walk in the room.) Mix two trays of color with glaze—white and warm off-white. Round sponges work well for clouds. Use the pure white to sponge on cumulous clouds—flatter on the bottom, rolling and rounded on the top. While the white is still workable, use the warm off-white to highlight the tops and sides of the clouds that are toward your imagined light source.

Mural, Mural on the Wall

Murals are very popular for rooms today. You can hire an artist for your murals, or use a "paint-by-number" technique. Murals are a wonderful way to bring creativity and ambience to a room. Muraling can be inexpensive as far as supplies

page 80   Great Spaces—Learning Places

(paint), but it does require a time commitment. I usually draw a sketch of what I want on the wall, and ask the artist to take it from there.

You may be fortunate to have a talented artist or two in your church. Some high school artists have contributed beautiful murals to the children's ministry areas in their churches. Ask the artist for pencil sketches. Sometimes a composite of ideas from two different sketches will end up being your choice. A color sketch comes next.

Believe it or not, you can do a sort of "paint by number" mural that can be quite beautiful. Find ideas from pictorial books of Israel, Bible story books and publications such as **National Geographic**. The Internet is a treasure trove of muraling resources. Check out www.muralsplus.com for great advice plus a photo gallery of thousands of completed murals. The artists at www.trompe-l-oeil-art.com give detail shots of beautiful murals and generously share step-by-step instructions for many of their techniques.

Painting murals on cinder block walls is tricky. Take a "Monet" approach. That loose, impressionist look doesn't require defined lines and shapes. A soft, blended look works well on such a rough surface.

Stenciling also works well. In one church, a volunteer made her own stencils mimicking the motif in the fabric I selected. I showed her where to place them on the wall and she stenciled them in. This particular motif was an abstract geometric that we used in a computer room and the geometric forms were connected by curved lines that gave

Fun Ways with Walls and Ceilings

the look of cable or computer wiring. I simply started connecting the forms with a magic marker, moving fluidly from form to form. It turned out great and very much like the fabric motif.

Dale Olsen of Olsen Studios in the Chicago area has done beautiful murals for children's ministry areas. One of Dale's unique approaches is to sketch a large scene on ceiling tiles. He numbers bottles of acrylic craft paint and areas on the drawing. Children in various classes work on the tiles with this paint-by-number approach. When each class finishes its section, they assemble the tiles and ooh and ah at their incredible work of art!

Dale's murals are instructional as well as beautiful. In one room he's covered walls with accurate maps of Bible lands. Down a hallway he's created a timeline of the Bible. Dale shares his advice on muraling in the section that follows.

Muraling Tips from Dale Olsen

When you're going to create a wall-sized work of art, begin by preparing the wall surface. (And you wanted it to be fun right away, didn't you?) Fill holes with spackle; sand and smooth. Then prime the wall with good quality, stain-hiding primer such as Bulls Eye or Kilz.

If you'll be painting on walls from which wallpaper has been removed, you'll need to apply two coats of solvent-based alkyd primer to seal in any remaining traces of wallpaper paste or adhesive.

Now the fun begins. It's time to put your design on the wall. There are several ways you can do that.

Method 1

Measure the wall and make a scale drawing of it on paper. You may want to use graph paper with three squares equaling one foot of wall. On plain paper, draw an inch for every foot of wall, or use any scale that's convenient for you. Then sketch the mural onto the scale drawing of the wall.

With your scale drawing in hand, draw the mural onto the wall with a pencil. You may draw a very light one-foot grid on the wall to assist you.

Method 2
Break down your sketch of the mural into smaller drawings and project them onto the wall with an opaque projector. Trace the projected image onto the wall with a pencil. Opaque projectors are available at art supply stores and catalogs. They will generally project images up to six inches square.

Method 3
Photograph a drawing of the mural with slide film, then use a slide projector to project it on the wall. Trace the image with a pencil. Slide photography also allows you to pose people as models in costume and project their images onto the wall. You may also project and trace slides of scenery. Building your mural with slides gives you great options for adding realistic detail even if you're not the world's greatest artist! Just pay attention to scale and perspective as you place the images together.

A Muralist's Supply List

- ☐ Pencils, H and 2H
- ☐ Art gum eraser
- ☐ Kneaded rubber eraser
- ☐ Sanding block or pad
- ☐ Ruler and yardstick
- ☐ Carpenter's level
- ☐ 45 degree drafting triangle
- ☐ Putty knife
- ☐ Spackle
- ☐ Paint stirrers
- ☐ T-square
- ☐ Mixing buckets with seals
- ☐ Disposable foam plates
- ☐ Plastic cups
- ☐ Blue painter's tape
- ☐ Latex gloves
- ☐ Paint trays
- ☐ Paint tray liners
- ☐ Foam and artists' brushes
- ☐ Roller & roller covers
- ☐ Sea and cellulose sponges
- ☐ Paper towels
- ☐ Clean rags
- ☐ Canvas drop cloths
- ☐ TEC stain remover
- ☐ Goof-Off 2™ cleaner
- ☐ Murphy's Oil Soap
- ☐ Trash bags

Fun Ways with Walls and Ceilings

All projection methods require a considerable distance between the projector and the wall plane. This method would not be suitable in an eight-foot wide corridor but works well in a 20-foot room. Remember that when you project an image, the lens should be in the center of the image to avoid distortion.

Method 4
If you have a full-size drawing of the mural, you can tape it to the wall, place transfer paper under it and trace the drawing with a pencil. You can purchase both dark and light transfer paper at art supply stores.

When I pack supplies for a muraling job, I take the kitchen sink—as you can see from my list. For a small scale job, you can get by with less. But it's always great to have a few extra tools at hand rather than stopping your work to hunt for what you need. Consider the size and scale of your job. If you're going to be working several feet off the ground, it's worth it to rent scaffolding or an adjustable ladder that forms a working platform. Extra lighting is handy, especially when the light in the room is minimal or shadowy in your work area.

Note also that decorative paint effects for imitating stone walls, leafy trees, stone paths, etc. can be achieved by using such common things as crumpled plastic dry cleaning bags, newspaper formed into a loose wrinkled ball, mop heads, kitchen sponges, carpet scraps (make sure these are washed to remove any lint) or anything else that has texture or bristles.

A Word About Brushes
Good brushes are worth the price. Really. Cheap brushes will give you sloppy edges and shed in your work. Artists' brushes can cost a great deal. For your detail work, a good quality craft brush will do nicely. Look for brands such as Robert Simmons, One Stroke™, Royal Langnickle™ and Loew Cornell™.

Acrylic paint dries in brushes quickly, and dried paint is very difficult to remove. If you're going to set a brush aside for a few minutes, place it in a jar of clean water. Clean your brushes often with good old soap and water. Scrub smaller brushes on the palm of your hand, then rinse thoroughly and reshape. Store artists' brushes flat or with the handle down, bristles up.

Sponge brushes are little workhorses that can save your more expensive brushes from wear and tear. They cut a decent edge and they're easy to clean. If paint dries in a sponge brush, apologize to it and toss it out.

Choosing Paint and Mediums

• Flat acrylic latex wall paint

You will paint large areas of your mural with flat acrylic latex wall paint. This is not the time to purchase the cheapest paint on the shelf. Go for a top quality name brand.

• Acrylic craft paints, 2 oz. bottles

You'll find a variety of craft paints at hobby and discount stores. Two of the most reliable are Delta Ceramcoat™ and Folk Art™ Acrylics. They come in every shade of the rainbow, so you can find just the colors you need. Resist the temptation to mix colors. You may be able to mix exactly the color you want, but you'll be in trouble when you need more of it. Keep in mind that paints in the bottle are lighter than dried paint on the wall.

• Artists' acrylic paint

Good quality artists' paints such as Golden, Liquitex or Winsor Newton, are much pricier than bottled craft paints. I use them in important areas of the mural. Their brilliance adds a big visual splash. Artists' acrylic product lines also offer extenders and retarders that can be mixed into the paint to slow drying times.

• Glazing medium

Adding glazing medium to paint slows the drying time. It allows you to blend the paint smoothly and to add glazes (thin layers) of paint to get rich colors and subtle shading. Every major paint manufacturer makes glazing medium. Through years of professional muraling, I have come to prefer the AQUA-GLAZE® brand. It is available from Faux Effects, Inc. of Vero Beach, FL and can be purchased online at www.fauxstore.com. I use AQUA-SEAL® from the same source. It is a seal coat that turns flat latex paint into an exceptional base coat. It can be applied over the finished work for maximum durability.

Let's Paint!

Mural drawn, drop cloths in place. Paints, brushes and tools at the ready on a worktable. You're wearing clothes and shoes that love the occasional splotch of color. Let's paint!

Block in the large areas with wall paints. Block in medium and small areas with craft paint. Don't worry about highlights and shadows at this point. Just put on a base coat so the whole mural is covered. Roll on two coats of water based clear sealer. This step will allow the next glazes to stay wet and workable for up to two hours. Without the sealer, the glaze would be sucked into previous layers of paint and dry too quickly.

Add details, light and shading to one section of the mural at a time. Use glazing medium to blend colors and achieve subtle shading of light to dark in objects such as clothing, leaves on trees, the gradation of light to dark in the sky and in making realistic looking clouds. Use fine quality artists' acrylic paints at key points in the mural for brilliant color.

Finishes

You'll need to protect the finished mural so the inevitable handprints can be cleaned without damaging the paint. I recommend the use of a clear product, water-based, in the "dull" or matte classification. A gloss finish highlights imperfections in the wall surfaces; a satin finish produces glare.

Remember to clean walls gently. Even with a protective top coat, no painted finish is truly scrubbable. They will all show wear and tear in areas where scrub brushes have been applied by a highly motivated person using lots of elbow grease.

Record Keeping

In the event that you may wish to repair damage or paint a similar mural elsewhere, keep a file for each painting that includes the color numbers of the latex paint and the color names of all craft paints and artist acrylics you used. Record which coatings were used and in which order, and the name of the finish topcoat you used. Include a "cut" sheet if you can obtain it. (A cut sheet is a data sheet put out by the manufacturer that gives a detailed product description.) You can also mark and save paint cans, which have valuable information on the label.

Chapter Seven

Structural Savvy—Safe and Up to Code

"The aim of art is to represent not the outward appearance of things, but their inward significance."
-Aristotle

Before we leave the design idea phase, we need to
cover issues of health, safety, comfort and building codes. If you've been inspired to tackle a major remodeling project with removal and replacement of walls, you'll probably work with an architect. You'll need a building permit from your city or village.

Safety is always a primary consideration
when you're creating spaces for children. Fabric needs to be treated with fire retardant. Use rounded corners rather than sharp ones. Trim dangling cords from blinds. Hallways must be clear of clutter—no paper, no clothing. Remove the coat racks from the hallway. And remove artwork from hallways walls in preschool environments. Unfortunately it's as dangerous as it is charming. Hallways are the primary fire escape route and it is extremely dangerous to have flammable items in the escape route. Some local fire codes only allow 10% flammable product in hallways. If you have decorative fabric awnings over market place murals (with flame retardant applied, of course), you've used up most of that 10%.

Structural Savvy—Safe and Up to Code

Know the Code

If you are making minor changes in an existing building, codes, standards and federal regulations must always be taken into consideration. Check with your municipality to be sure you are meeting codes for accessibility, plumbing, mechanical, life safety (fire protection), electrical, and performance levels of HVAC (heating, ventilation, and air conditioning).

There may be other local codes specific to your area you will need to know about. Contact your local fire marshal and building inspector to learn about them.

Causes of poor IAQ can include:
- poor mechanical systems and ventilation
- lack of proper humidity and moisture control
- inadequate housekeeping and product control
- outdoor pollutants and vehicle exhaust.

Hot, Cold or Just Right?

Like the porridge Goldilocks chose, the temperature in children's rooms needs to be just right. This can be a challenge, because temperature control poses problems in many church buildings. The temperature may vary greatly from one room to the next. If the building is regulated by central heating controls, rooms may lack individual thermostats. Temperatures that are too cool affect dexterity. In rooms that are too hot, children's attentiveness decreases. If you're about the business of tearing into walls, it's a perfect time to make necessary adjustments to the heating system.

Indoor Air Quality

A growing body of evidence now links poor health with poor Indoor Air Quality in both students and teachers. Symptoms may range from mild to acute. Studies by the EPA show that Poor

page 88 Great Spaces—Learning Places

IAQ may impair a person's ability to do tasks requiring concentration, calculation and memory (EPA, 2003). Among the leading illnesses associated with poor IAQ are asthma and respiratory infections.

Poor indoor air quality directly affects students' health. Children in "sick buildings" have been found to exhibit allergies, skin rashes and mental fatigue. When ventilation is poor, carbon monoxide can rise to dangerous levels without anyone being aware of the problem. In this situation children may experience decreased concentration, drowsiness and headaches. In buildings where poor ventilation is an issue, by all means install CO_2 alarms in each room.

For further information, order the "IAQ Tools for Schools" kit from the EPA. You may order the kit by phone at 1-800-438-4318, by fax at 703-356-6386 or by writing to EPA Kit, PO Box 37133, Washington, DC 20013-7133.

Fire Retardancy

Over the years many tragic fires have been accelerated by flammable finishes and upholstery. Building codes stipulate the finishes necessary to reduce the possibility of a piece of fabric, wall covering, furniture or other finishes igniting. Fabrics, finishes and furniture are given a fire rating. Check with your local fire marshal for the rating requirements for your locality. Remember, local codes supersede all other codes.

For safety, all fabric used within the children's areas of churches needs to be treated with a fire retardant fabric seal. This can be applied by a fabric finishing company before the fabric is sewn into its application. It can also be applied after fabrication by using a spray product, IF there is a spray product that meets your local fire codes.

A fire retardant fabric seal spray product is available from Ballantyne Flame Proofing, 3230 Sprucewood Lane, Wilmette, IL 60091-1111. You may contact them by phone at 847-251-1899 or by fax at 847-251-1001. Their product meets or exceeds these criteria:
- NFPA #701
- Title 19 California Code (Section 1237.1)
- Fed. Std. 16DFR (FF 4-72) (mattress)
- FAR 25853B (Aircraft Materials)
- ASTM #-84 (glue down)

Plumbing

Cooking, science and art classrooms need a sink. The sink should have a minimum of 18" of counter space on each side.

Ergonomics

Ergonomics refers to physical comfort in performing tasks. Good ergonomics are important to children's growing bodies. Poor ergonomics can result in back strain, headaches and poor back development. We need to plan our spaces and our lessons so that children can be mobile. God made kids to move and explore his world with their bodies. Movement keeps them alert and engaged. Within a workshop period, children may sit on floor cushions, move about the room, move to a bench or stool or observe from a loft. This kind of movement actually improves learning and short term memory. Keeping kids still for an hour is not the proper goal! In your design plan, keep in mind flexibility in furnishings, scale appropriate for age and size, and areas for movement.

Lighting

Architectural and design studies show that environmental lighting has profound biological effects on people. Increased lighting in the environment alleviates depression, lessens fatigue, and increases learning proficiency. We want to provide as much natural daylight as possible. However, artificial lighting has come a long way since the day of green, buzzing fluorescent lights.

Children in standard institutional lighting are more fidgety and pay less attention than those in rooms with full-spectrum lighting. Full spectrum lighting helps students remain calm and interested in their work; there is less tendency toward hyperactivity. As you design your children's spaces, provide as much natural light as possible. Use full-spectrum lighting in fixtures. You can buy full-spectrum fluorescent lighting for standard fixtures.

You may want to add task lighting near study tables and computers. Then add accent lighting (ambient lighting) to the rooms. This may be track or stages, or may be floor lighting on tri-pods. Tripods in drama, puppet and musical performance areas not only add appropriate light—they also add a sense of theatrical design. A good source for theatrical lighting is One Way Street, Inc. Contact them at www.onewaystreet.com or 303-790-1188.

In computer rooms, do remember that the monitor's screen should not face a light source or a bright surface. The lighting in the room must not be brighter or darker than the screen or as the person looks up and down.

page 92 Great Spaces—Learning Places

Constantly adjusting to an environment lighter or darker than the screen causes eye fatigue. Ceiling lighting should come from an angle between 30 degrees and 60 degrees for glare-free light on computers. This means that if you have existing ceiling fixtures, you will want to place your computer table layout within that 30-60 degree angle range.

Draw a ceiling plan for your lighting in the same way you drew your floor plan. Draw in your lighting fixtures and hanging objects. Draw the outside walls and any cabinetry or built-ins that touch the ceiling. Ask your builder/contractor/architect to provide the lighting plan for the room and draw in those specified sources.

The Noise Factor

When you plan the shell of your rooms (walls, floor, ceiling and windows), be sure to plan for noise control. Children need low-noise classrooms. Noisy environments can cause deficits in mental concentration and limit children's processing abilities.

Imagine reading a book in which several words are dropped from each sentence. It wouldn't take you long to lose interest and give up. That's exactly what happens to children in noisy classrooms. Adults can fill in the blanks. Younger children cannot predict from context what's missing.

The best way to limit general, ambient noise is through interior design. Sound absorbing materials for walls, floors, ceilings and furniture contribute greatly to reducing noise levels. Noise reducing measures include adding carpet and specially rated noise reduction suspended ceiling tiles. Fabric and upholstered furnishing also absorb sound. You may want to add "white noise" to mask distractions. White noise can be as simple as a fan running in the background or soft music or nature sounds on a CD.

page 94   Great Spaces—Learning Places

Chapter Eight

Work Your Plan

"Every great work of art has two faces, one toward its own time and one toward the future, toward eternity."

— Daniel Barenboim

With all the decision making done, the plans in writing and in drawings, it's time to work your plan. Who will purchase the products, paint the walls, build needed elements, sew and install window treatments, put in new flooring and complete all the myriad tasks ahead?

Every church has a different design plan—there is no "one size fits all" set of instructions. But these general implementation tips will guide you through the process.

Create time lines and schedule installations on your calendar. Plan "Saturday Volunteer Days" and blitz the place! Planning prior to this stage is essential so that all supplies are available when that very valuable volunteer force shows up! I have one word for you:

SPREADSHEETS!

Recruiting

Creative recruiting will produce a varied and energetic force of volunteers. In some churches, adult Sunday school classes or Bible study groups adopt rooms to complete. This turns out to be a productive and fun effort and results in a great camaraderie. University Christian Church in Fort Worth, Texas reported that a total of 144 volunteers worked over the course of five weeks, totaling 3,300 hours of labor to make "Journey Land" the wonderful place that it is.

Consider taping a recruiting video. Have it running after church in a highly visible area. Place a sign-up sheet next to it. University Christian Church in Fort Worth put together a promotional video of their children's program development that you can purchase. Contact: Minister of Christian Education, University Christian Church, 2720 South University Drive, Ft. Worth, TX 76109.

Create a tasteful display of drawing and plans. Intersperse photos of children in your ministry. Make a sign-up sheet part of the display. Be sure to have spaces where people can list their availability and contact information.

Don't forget the teenagers and college kids in your congregation. You're likely to have some skilled artists and workers in that group, and they love to take on a service challenge together.

Set your dates, invite your volunteers to a day of work and fun, bring in pizza for lunch and watch your design come alive!

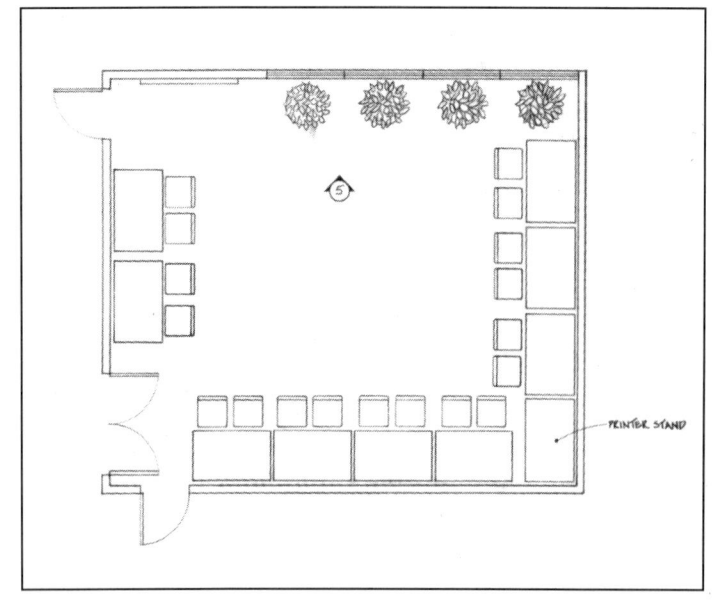

Fund Raising and Purchasing

If you will need to raise funds for your design implementation, put together a list of everything you need and display the list in the church next to the drawings of your new area. Show the fabric swatches, carpet selection and wall designs. Then ask people if they will donate toward the project. Ask, "Would you donate $25 toward a can of paint?" or "Would you donate $300 toward the purchase of theme-based fabric?" As donations come in,

Great Spaces—Learning Places

cross those items off your list with bright red marker. The crossed-off items can serve as a visual display of your fund raising progress.

I've learned that it's best for one knowledgeable person to do the purchasing. This will ensure getting exactly the right pieces rather than disappointing substitutes. Have all materials purchased and ready for your labor force to work on when they come in, along with floor plans, elevations, and written explanations of the work to be done in the room. Tape your Classroom Specification Worksheets and all the drawings outside the door of each classroom.

Schedule and Sequence

Make a spreadsheet of work days and projects to be done. If, for example, you have decided to work as a team every Saturday in the summer, assign specific tasks to each Saturday. The first Saturday in June will be clean-out day. Take down all bulletin boards and black boards, all decorative items, old window treatments, and remove the furniture you won't be keeping.

Work on your rooms needs to be completed from the top down. After clean-out, begin wiring and built-ins. Complete any wiring that's going to be hidden in the ceiling, then paint the ceiling. Old ceiling tiles that show watermarks or chips detract from the design of the room. Painting these with a roller is very easy and gives a surprising boost to your room.

It's wonderful to blend your ceiling into the theme of the room with faux sky and clouds. If you'll be hanging décor from dropped ceilings, purchase special clips from a hardware store. Tacking with a heavy-duty stapler works well on wallboard ceilings, but on tile drop ceilings the staples pull out too easily.

With wiring and built-ins finished, tackle the walls. Plan to wash the rooms down and apply primer one week and begin the final painting the next. Install flooring last. Take great care to protect your painted walls from being grazed by the edge of carpet rolls.

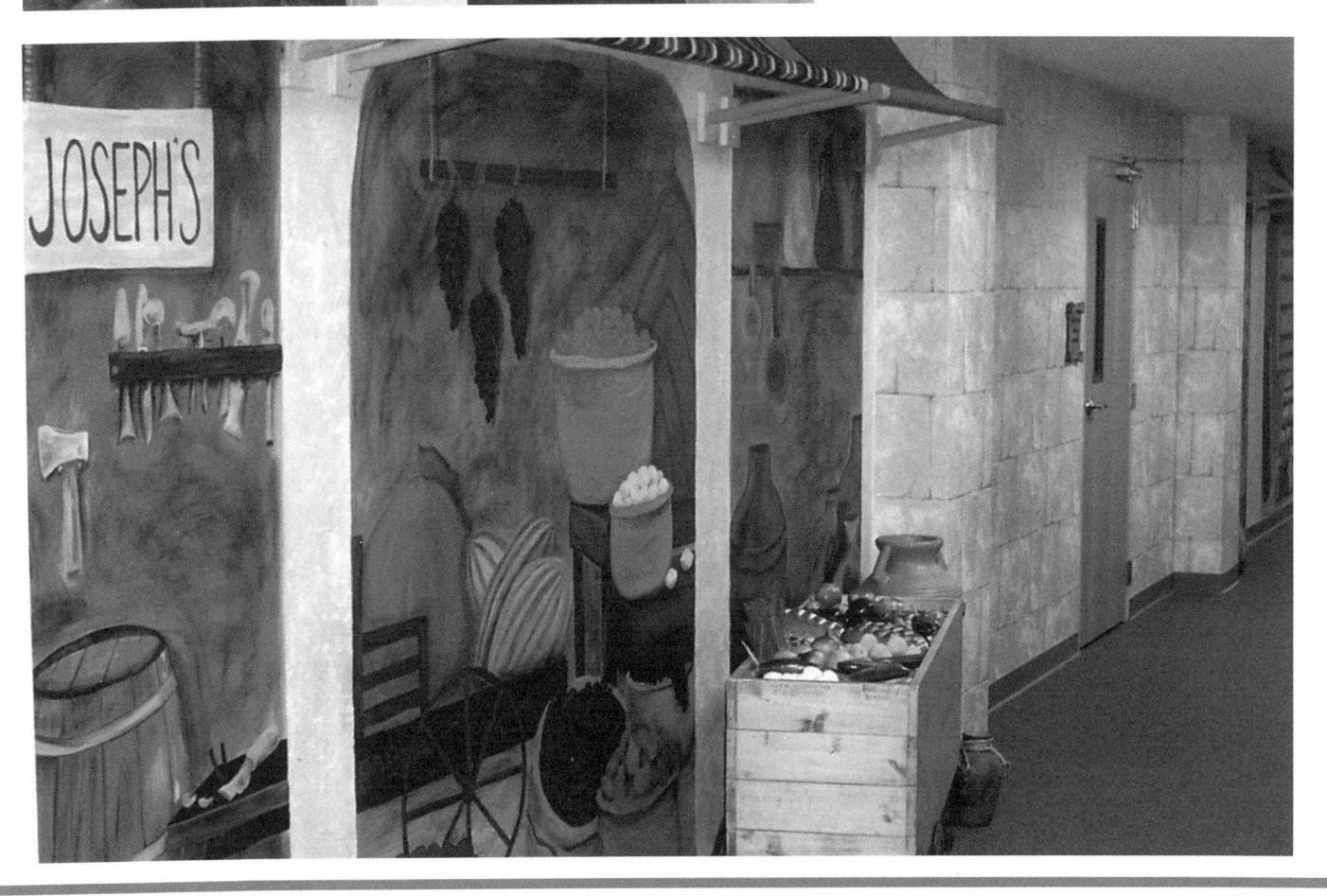

Work Your Plan   page 99

Gathering Donated Accessories

The first step is to put a "wish list" in your church newsletter and as a bulletin insert. Be specific—one church asked for a camel saddle and ended up getting not one, but two! Do you want oriental rugs? Often people have old ones they will be glad to give. Have them cleaned and layer them for the floor of a tent. Do you want baskets and pottery? For an old world look the baskets need to be rustic. You want Middle Eastern pottery, not Mexican or Roman.

Help everyone understand that you're fleshing out very specific themes. Explain that you'll be glad to look at the accessories people offer, but if the items don't work with your design plan, ask them not to be offended.

Furnishings

If you're recycling furniture, plan to have volunteers paint or upholster it on your work days. You may ask someone who's handy to build low tables. Floor pillows work well as seating with tables that are 18 inches tall. If you've located creative seating such as barrels or benches, use volunteers to sand and finish them.

Signage

Replacing signage is important and is regulated by building codes for safety. Remember that signs cannot hang down from ceiling lower than 80 inches off the floor. Signs that hang from the wall and protrude into the hallway must also be above the 80-inch mark. If they are lower than that, they can protrude a maximum of four inches. Signs may hang from the ceiling or be attached to the wall next to the door on the door-knob side.

Work Your Plan

Recruit your best craftspeople to create signage. Their workmanship will be a central component of your overall design, seen week after week by people who may never even enter the workshop rooms. Be sure graphics are bold enough to be seen clearly from a distance.

Cheerleader, Critic, Coach

Wait on God and ask him to help you fulfill all of the these roles. You want the creation of this children's ministry area to be fondly remembered by everyone involved. As the wise saying goes, "many hands make light work," so recruit and recruit. This is a rare opportunity to bring together people who wouldn't otherwise know each other. As the weeks go by and people see how fun this project is, you'll gain help.

> Keep the big picture in front of everyone—including yourself!

You'll need to be gentle but firm in guarding the quality of the work. Be sure to say tons of thank yous, praise the volunteer work, surprise everyone with doughnuts, and, in general, be the cheerleader for your team. When you hit a rough spot, step back and point out how far you've come. Keep the big picture in front of everyone—including yourself!

Chapter Nine

Jubilee! Celebration and Evaluation

"At the dedication of the wall of Jerusalem, the Levites were sought out from where they lived and were brought to Jerusalem to celebrate joyfully the dedication with songs of thanksgiving and with the music of cymbals, harps and lyres."
— Nehemiah 12:27

Completing a project of this size definitely calls for a grand celebration.
As a matter of fact, it calls for three celebrations: one for the workers before the children see it, then the grand opening week for the children, followed by an open house for the parents.

Job Well Done Party

Have your new space completed a few days before you introduce the kids to it. Plan a party for your design team. Walk through the entire area together and explain again the vision of each room. Serve progressive refreshments—a little something in each room so everyone gets to see the finished rooms as they snack. Make a large sign with your "Angels" listed on it—a thank you to everyone who participated in this renovation. Have your senior pastor help you give public thank yous. Close with a prayer of dedication, then invite everyone to come attend the Grand Opening with the children.

Angel List
- Kim
- Tom
- Nancy
- Joe

Evaluation Form

Evaluator _____ Date _____

Room _____

1. Rate overall aesthetic appeal: 1 2 3 4 5
   Suggestions/Comments _____
   _____
   _____

2. Safety Issues (note any concerns you have by room)

   Physical concerns/hazards_____
   _____

   Thermal quality_____
   _____

   Other_____
   _____

3. Use of space and flow of traffic with children in room.
   Rate: Fair   Good   Excellent

   Suggestions/Comments_____
   _____

4. Other comments_____
   _____
   _____

Permission to photocopy this evaluation sheet granted for local church use. Copyright © Cook Communications Ministries. Published in *Great Spaces, Learning Places* by Jan Hubbard.

Grand Opening

I recommend that the children not be allowed into the area during the construction of your design. Let them anticipate the excitement of seeing it for the first time on opening Sunday.

At one church, as the "The Kingdom" children's area was being constructed, the children met in the fellowship hall for summer Sunday school. All summer long the Christian Education Director reminded them, "The Kingdom is coming! The Kingdom is coming!" Their excitement grew and grew until opening day when they burst through the "golden gates" into "The Kingdom" at the top of the stairs. Their eyes were wide, smiles burst on their faces and they raised their arms to cheer. Their sense of wonder was a blessing for all as they experienced this new place for the first time through all their senses—the twinkling stars on the ceiling, the tantalizing smells from the popcorn machine where signs directed them to Cinemas I and II, the happy welcome songs sung and choreographed by puppets at the new puppet stage. It was pure sensory delight! And we knew this was just the beginning of all the marvelous adventure that lay ahead as they came to know God and his Word. That was something to celebrate!

> Their sense of wonder was a blessing for all as they experienced this new place for the first time through all their senses.

Jubilee! Celebration and Evaluation

If your church plans to renovate just one room at a time, celebrate the opening of each room. Tape "Under Construction" banners across the doorways of rooms that are in progress. On the Sunday when you're ready to open a room, make it a special occasion for the children.

Open House for Adults

After the children have enjoyed opening day, hold an open house when all the adults of the church can visit the rooms. You may want to make it the following Sunday, or perhaps a month into your new program. Have a teacher or coordinator in each room to explain the décor and teaching that is done in that room. Let children act as hosts and hostesses, serving small refreshments in each room.

Give your Open House a theme that is tied to your program theme. One church called its children's program "God's Garden" and invited everyone to "The Garden Party" open house. If your program is called "Journey Land," have a "Bon Voyage Party." Bring some more of that creativity you used to design your space into celebrating the open house. Have shepherds wear their Bible time attire, crank the popcorn machine and give everyone a first hand taste of the wonderful things in store for the children in your ministry!

Follow Up

After the open house, reconvene your design group and evaluate what you've observed so far. What's working great? What needs tuning up? What doesn't quite work as planned? Any unforeseen safety issues? These must be corrected immediately.

As you process your observations, develop recommendations for improvements and future projects. List and prioritize your concerns and your wish lists (back to that strategic planning!), because if you don't write things down and give them a date, chances are they won't get done. Work on refining your design over the next few months.

Down the Road

One question I'm often asked is, "How long will this work last?" First, I doubt that we will ever return to the classroom look we had in the last century. As our understanding of how children learn has progressed, so has our motivation to create enriched environments.

> As our understanding of how children learn has progressed, so has our motivation to create enriched environments.

Suppose a little boy has a race car theme in his bedroom. Dad built a bed that looks like a race car, the window treatments look like the start flags and small race cars are pictured all over the wallpaper. This boy lives in this room every day for years and years before that theme gets changed.

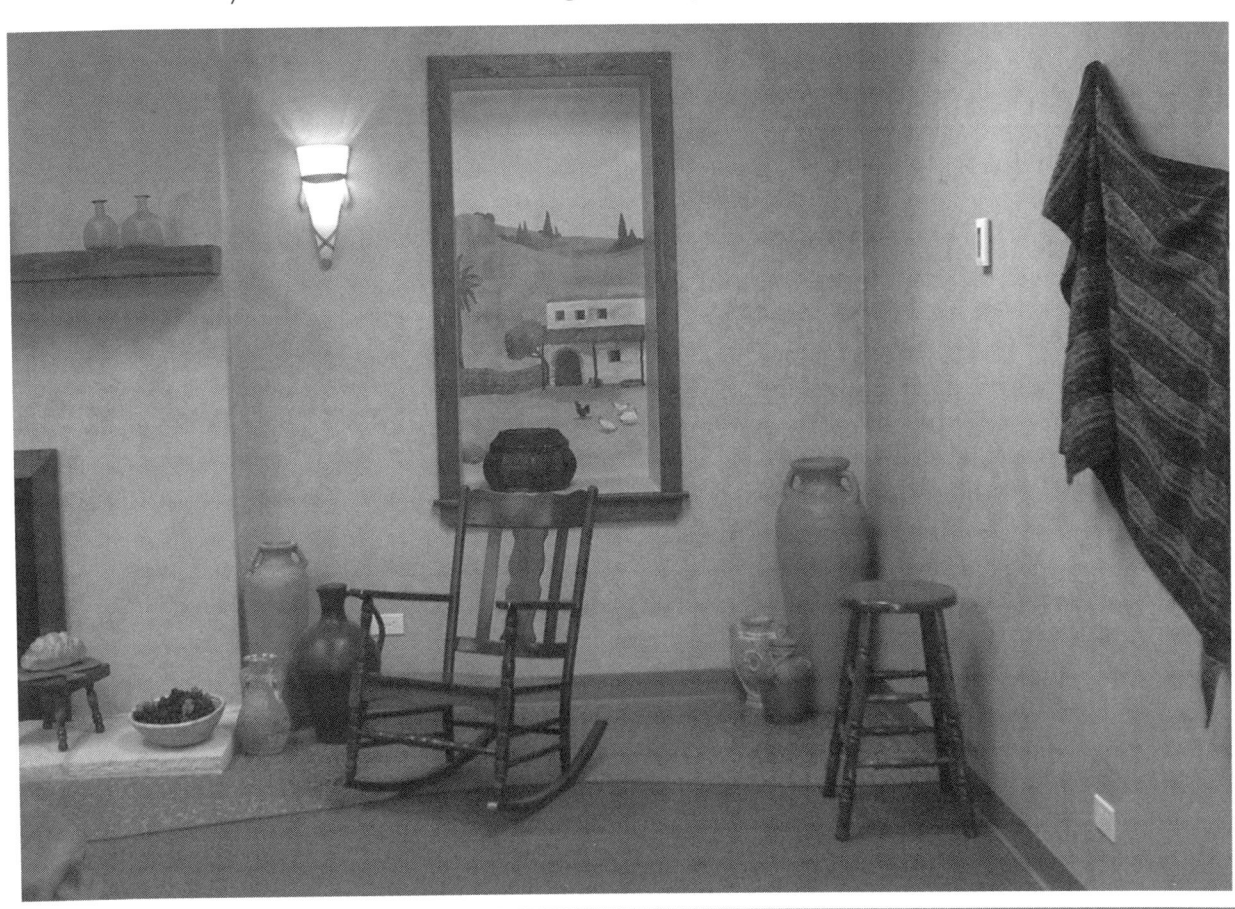

Jubilee! Celebration and Evaluation

We have children coming into our church themed rooms once or twice a week during their growing up years. And the rooms change as they get older. As an example, they begin in "Noah's Ark" nursery, go on to "Little Lambs" for preschool, to "Whale Tales" for kindergarten and to rooms with a "Faith Explorer's" theme for their elementary years. The junior and senior high school ages each have their own "chat rooms" (a room for Bible study and discussion) and then enjoy sharing a great recreation room with musical instruments, a ping pong table and a small kitchen for pizza night snacking. Kids enjoy their learning time the rooms and anticipate their progression to the next levels. If these rooms are well built and maintained, you can count on them to last for years and years.

Walk in Wonder

The awe that children experience when they see their learning space for the first time holds a great lesson for us all. Like a child, be aware of your senses. Make a choice to look at things as if you're seeing them for the first time. Take joy in the small delights God sprinkles into your day. Cultivate a grateful heart as you see the work of God's loving hand. Notice. Marvel. Be fascinated and amazed.

> The awe that children experience when they see their learning space for the first time holds a great lesson for us all.

You've dreamed up and brought into existence a place of wonder where children can grow in their experience of God. You've given them a place to slow them down, become aware of their surrounding, perceive God's truth through all their senses and wonder at his love for them. And they will never forget it!

Appendix

Meet the Author

Jan has been interested in Christian education since she volunteered to help in the church nursery as a girl. As a teenager she was active in the choir and youth group; later she became a group leader, Sunday school teacher, and Christian Education Elder. She feels blessed to be able to blend her career in interior design with her lifelong passion for Christian Education

After gaining a strong business foundation by conducting workshops in Marketing and Training and Development for sales organizations, Jan returned to school to acquire her degree in Interior Design. With this expertise she has been able to work in the areas of business development with design firms, strategic planning of enriched learning environments for Sunday schools as well as traditional Sunday School design and residential and contract interior design. She is a member of the American Society of Interior Designers and is NCIDQ Certified. Jan also teaches design classes at William Rainey Harper College in Palatine, IL.

Jan Hubbard, A.S.I.D., Interior Designer

As head of Design Directions for Church School based in Northbrook, Illinois, Jan has developed themes, designs and space planning for church Sunday schools across the country. She serves as a member of a national cooperative network to promote and support multidimensional learning in Sunday schools using the rotation model.

Design Directions for Church School, Ltd. provides:
- Creative space planning
- Biblical themes
- Unique wall and window treatments
- Color selection and coordination
- Lighting system plans
- Carpet and floor design
- Artwork and accessories

Design Directions for Church School, Ltd.

Design Directions for Church School, Ltd.
1524 Shermer Road, Northbrook, IL 60062
Web site: churchschooldesign.com
Email: churchschooldesign@yahoo.com
Phone 847-564-0676 Fax 847-564-3058

No matter where you are in the process—seeker, implementer, experienced Workshop Rotation educator or traditional Sunday School ready for a new look—Design Directions for Church School, Ltd. offers the right services for your church. Please visit our website at churchschooldesign.com for a complete overview of our work. Use the order form on the following page to order a free information packet.

"With Jan's advice, expertise and guidance, the Rotation Model became a reality for our church!"
   Kay Williams, Director of Children & Program Ministries, Atlanta, GA

Product Order Form

Design Directions for Church School, Ltd.

Order from Design Directions for Church School, Ltd.
1524 Shermer Road, Northbrook, IL 60062
847-564-0676
Fax 847-564-3058
E-mail: churchschooldesign@yahoo.co

		QUANTITY
Information Packet on Services & Fees	FREE!	_____
CD: "Interior Design for Sunday School Rooms" Pictures of rooms we have designed. Philosophy behind our design and steps to take to coordinate your design project. Great introduction for your congregation to upgrading your children's spaces.	$14.99	_____
Art Pyramid Drawings Construction drawings to make a portable art storage cart for supplies. Good for multiple use space—can be stored out of room when not in use.	$49.99	_____
Drama Wall Drawings (Portable) Construction drawings for drama wall on wheels. Drama backgrounds on one side; costume storage on the back. Good for multiple use space—can be stored out of room when not in use.	$49.99	_____
Puppet Stage Drawings (Upholstered) Constructions drawings for wooden structure that can be upholstered with theme related fabric over batting.	$49.99	_____
Loft Construction drawings for built-in loft.	$49.99	_____
Game Board Construction drawings for lighted wall game board for Bible knowledge games. Categories to choose from, degree of difficulty associated with the points awarded.	$59.99	_____
TOTAL		_____

Great Spaces—Order Form

Mural Artist

Dale Olsen

Dale Olsen of Olsen Studios, Inc. contributed the muraling section of Chapter 6.

Dale got his start by drawing on church bulletins and today occasionally paints his interpretation of the teaching Scripture during worship services in his church.

An accomplished artist in oils, acrylic and watercolor, Dale has had his work included in the inaugural national exhibition of the Oil Painters of America and has received honorable mention for landscape painting from the Artist's Magazine.

An architect, Dale began his faux finishing and mural painting business after volunteering to paint a mural for his church's Sunday School. His mural work and faux finishing have been published in *Chicago Home and Garden* magazine and *Decorate With Paint* magazine.

He resides with his wife and their teenage son in Clarendon Hills, Illinois

OLSEN STUDIOS, INC.

Murals
Faux Finishes
Trompe L'Oeil
Fine Art

Dale Olsen
123 Arthur Ave. Clarendon Hills, IL 60514
Phone/Fax (630) 654-3671

page 112 Mural Artist

Multi-Purpose Room

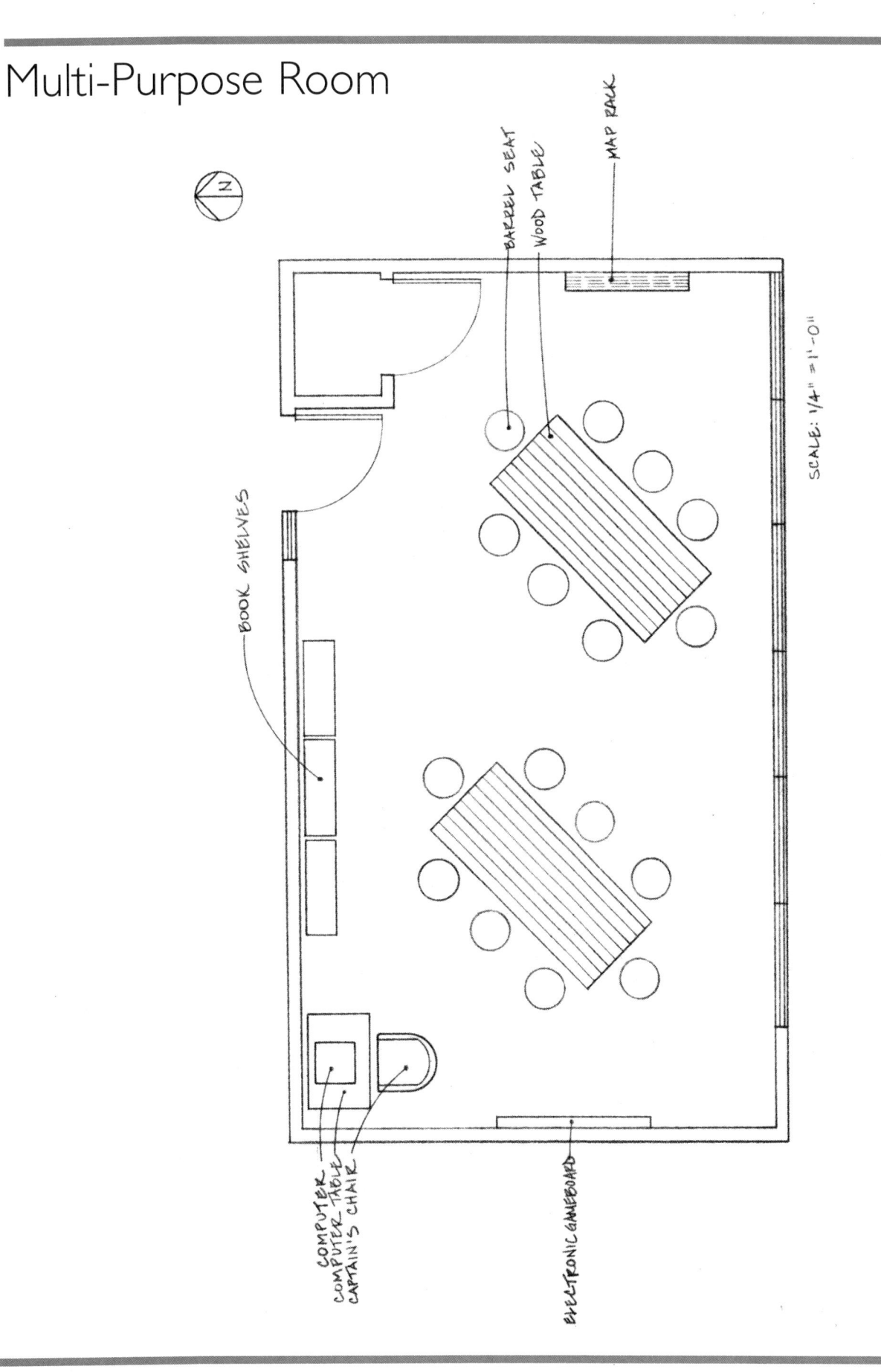

Appendix   page 113

How to Make a Canvas Awning

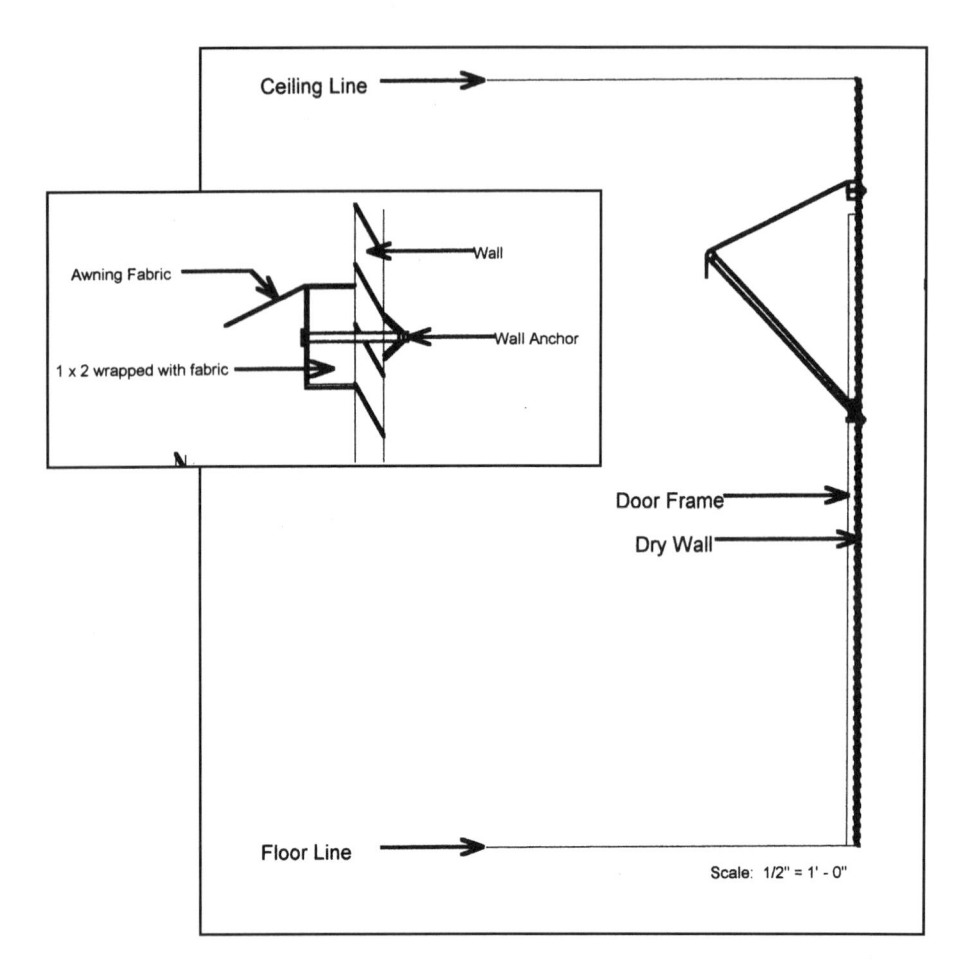

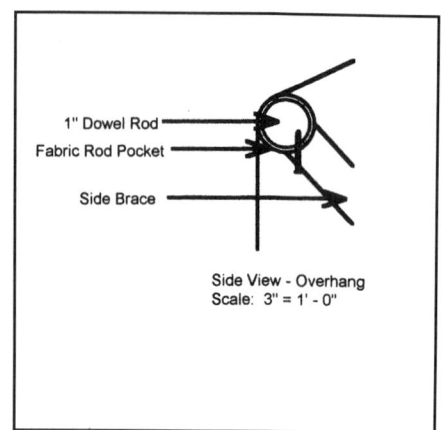

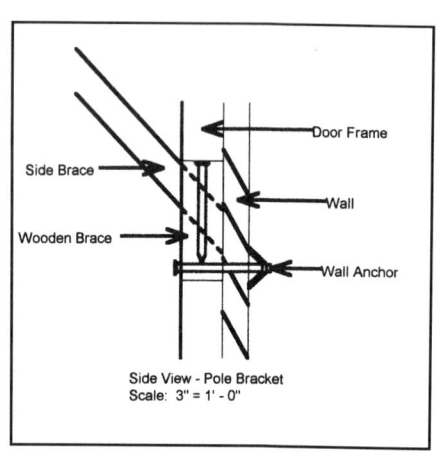

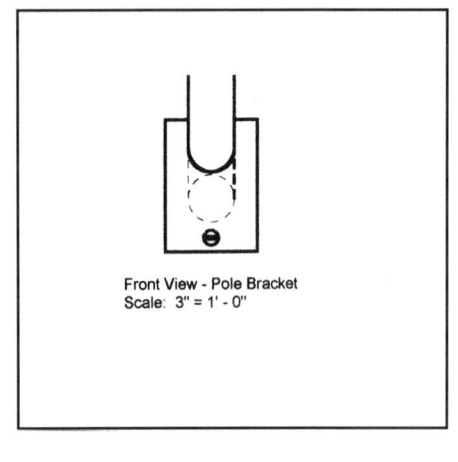

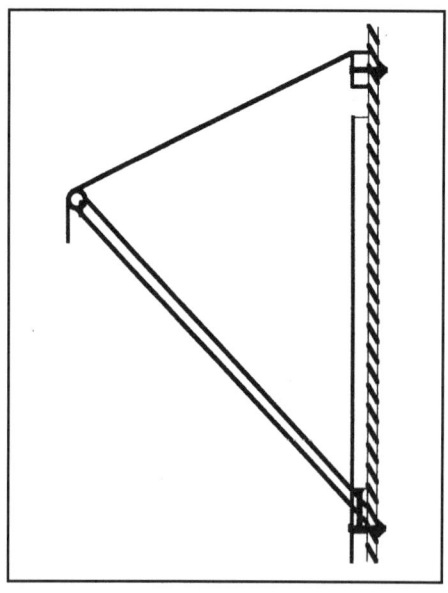

Ceiling Line

Awning Fabric
Wall
Wall Anchor
1 x 2 wrapped with fabric

Door Frame
Dry Wall

Floor Line

Scale: 1/2" = 1' - 0"

1" Dowel Rod
Fabric Rod Pocket
Side Brace

Side View - Overhang
Scale: 3" = 1' - 0"

Door Frame
Side Brace
Wall
Wooden Brace
Wall Anchor

Side View - Pole Bracket
Scale: 3" = 1' - 0"

Front View - Pole Bracket
Scale: 3" = 1' - 0"

page 114 Great Spaces—Learning Places

Computer Room 1

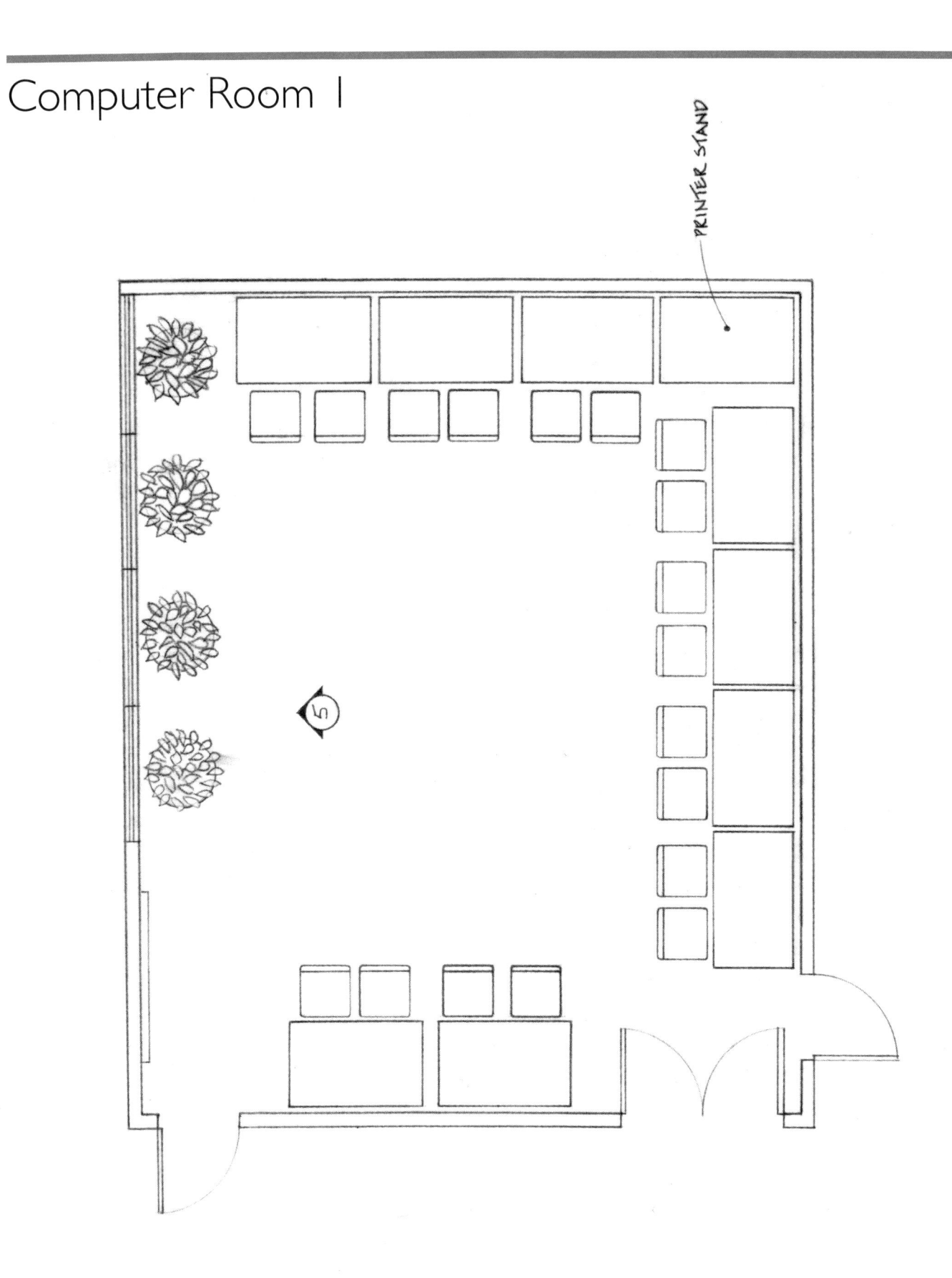

Appendix — page 115

Window Treatment

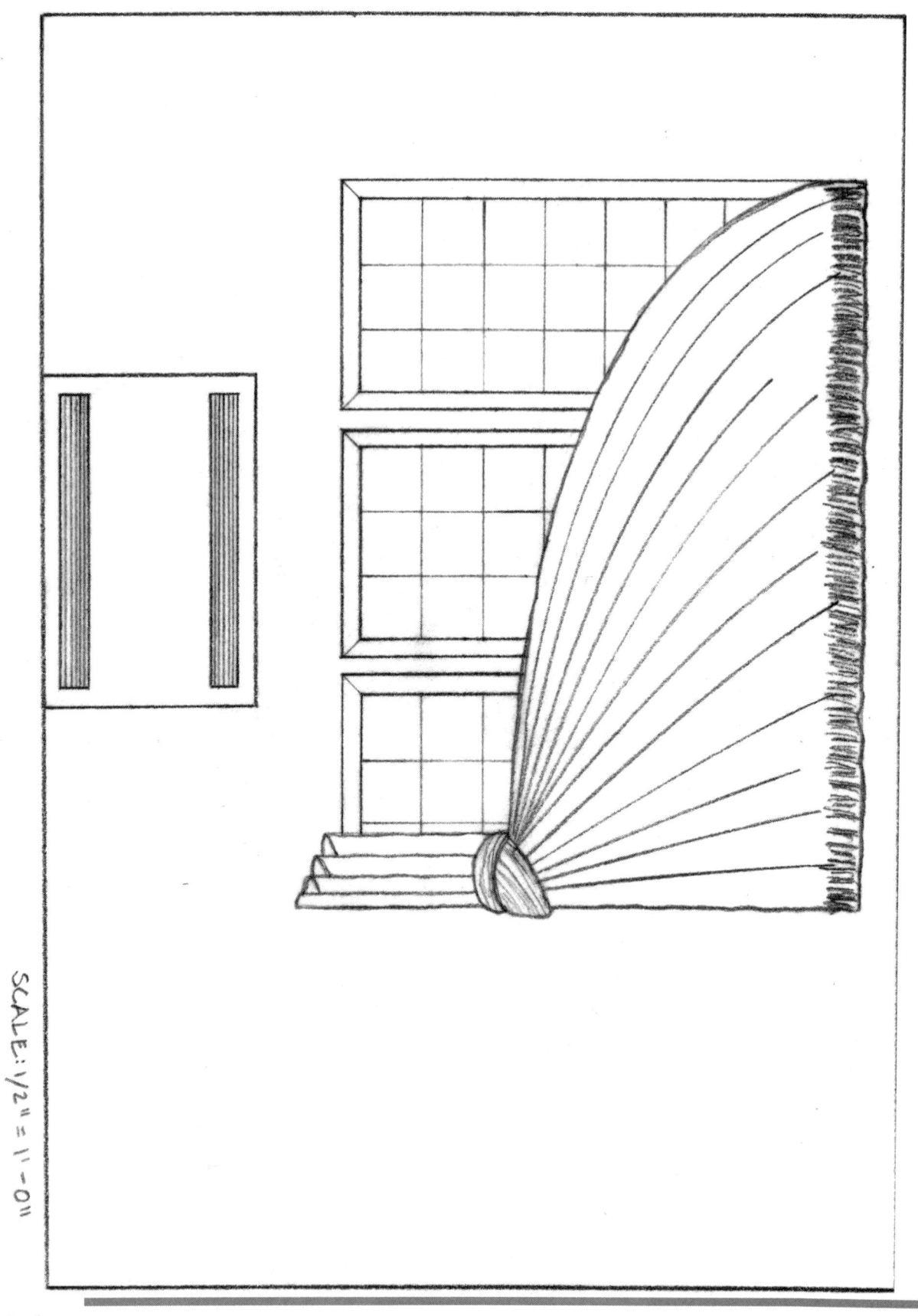

SCALE: 1/2" = 1'-0"

page 116 Great Spaces—Learning Places

Mural Sketch

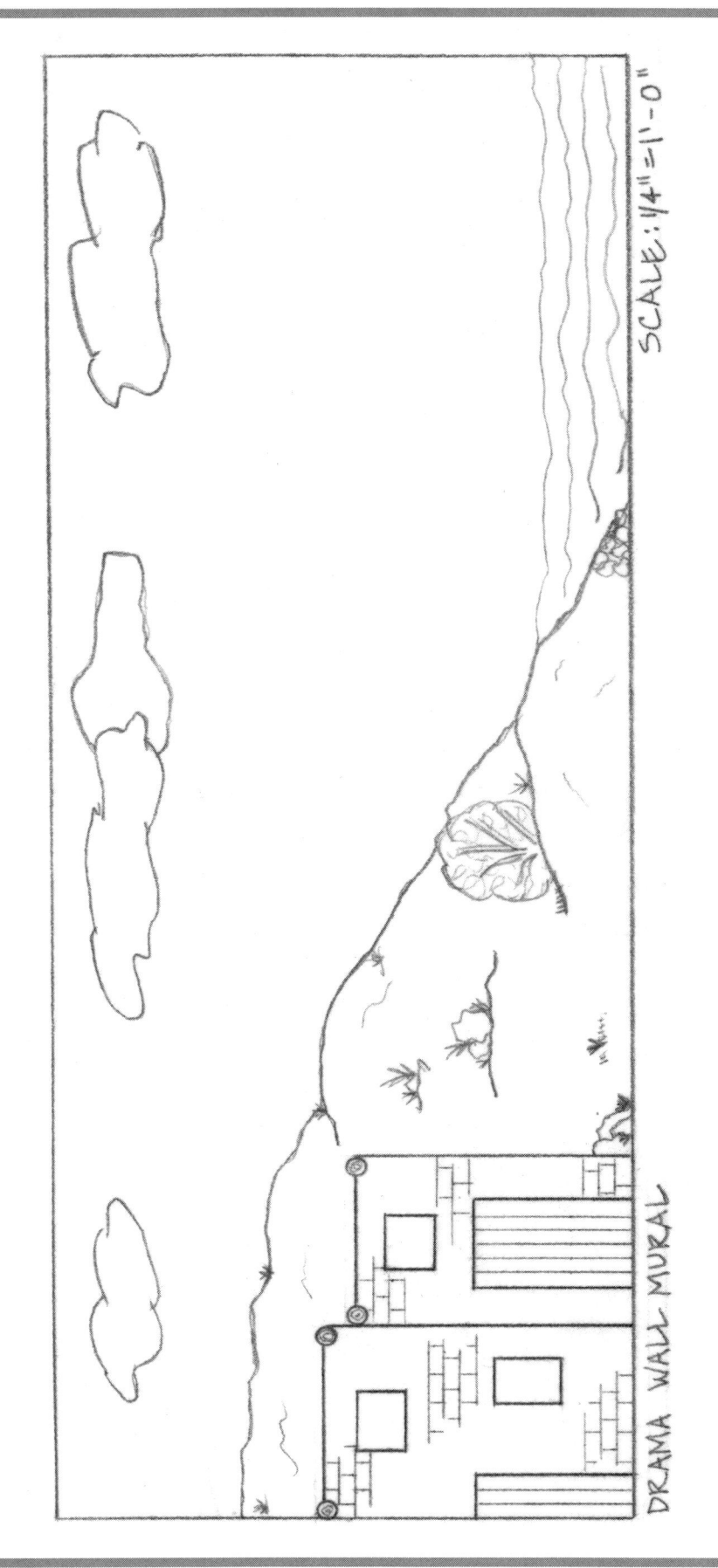

Appendix — page 117

Hallway

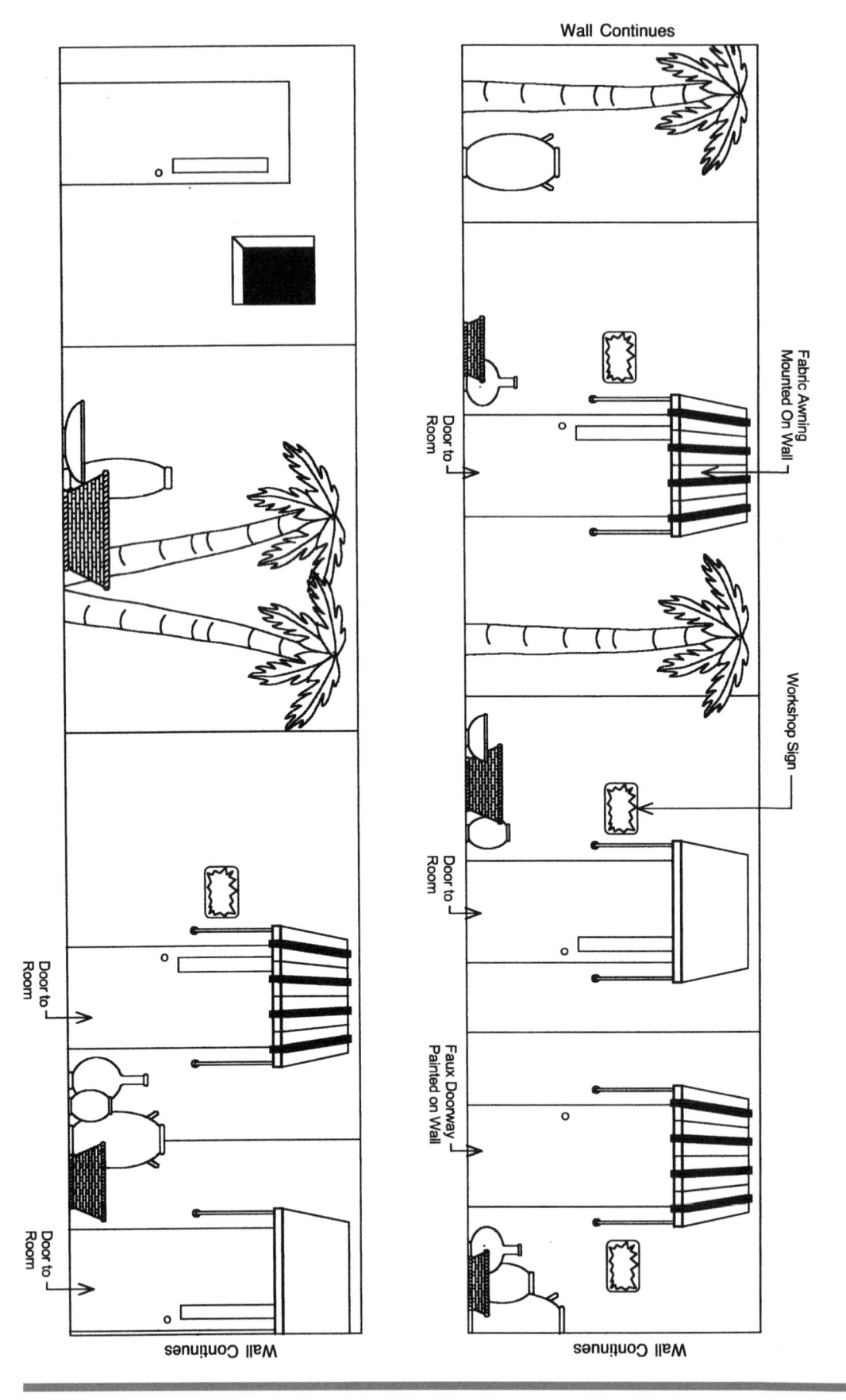

Wall Continues

Fabric Awning Mounted On Wall

Door to Room

Workshop Sign

Door to Room

Door to Room

Faux Doorway Painted on Wall

Door to Room

Wall Continues

Wall Continues

page 118 Great Spaces—Learning Places

Loft Room

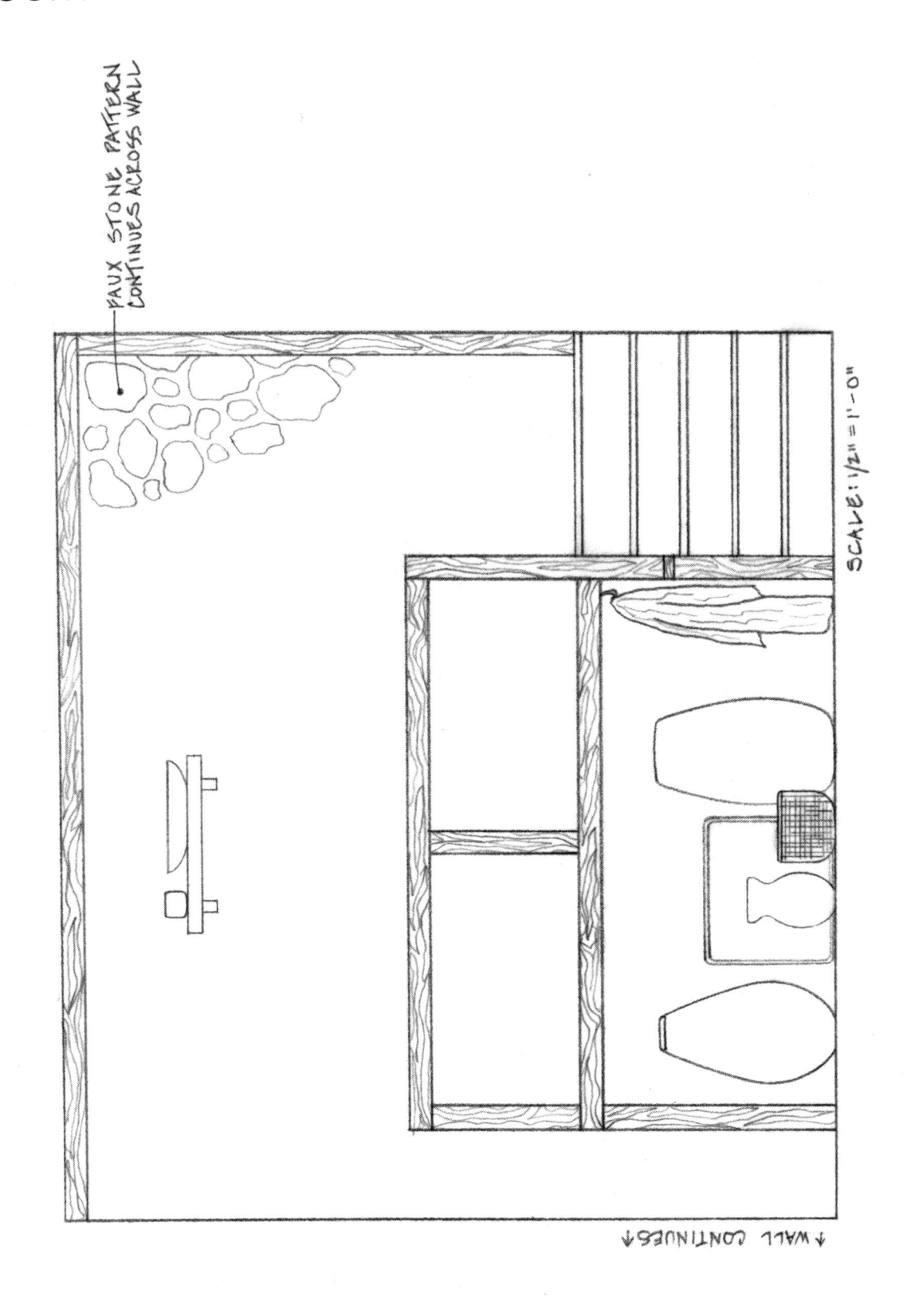

FAUX STONE PATTERN CONTINUES ACROSS WALL

SCALE: 1/2" = 1'-0"

↓ WALL CONTINUES ↓

Appendix   page 119

Market Place Sign

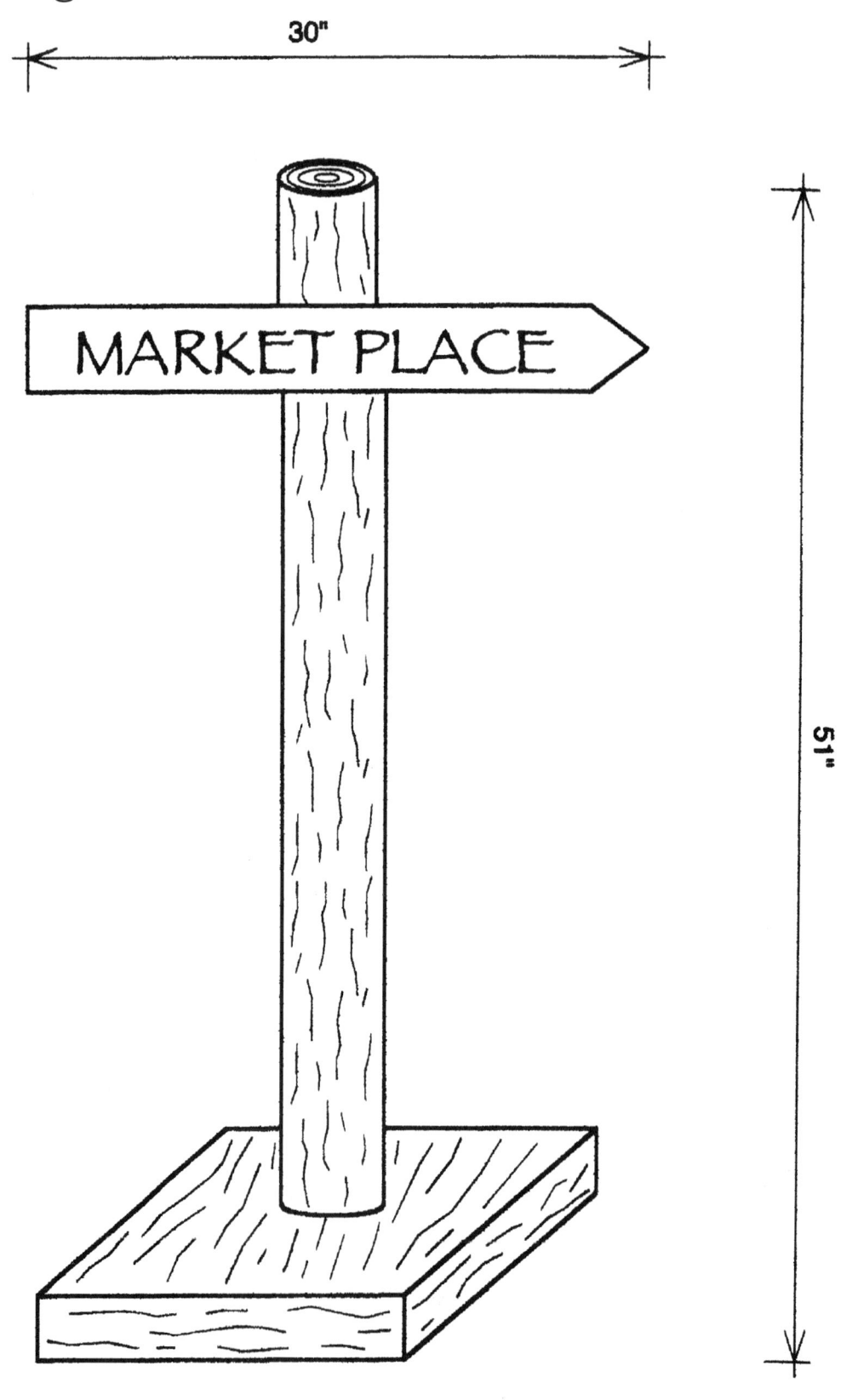

30"

51"

page 120 Great Spaces—Learning Places

Upper Room

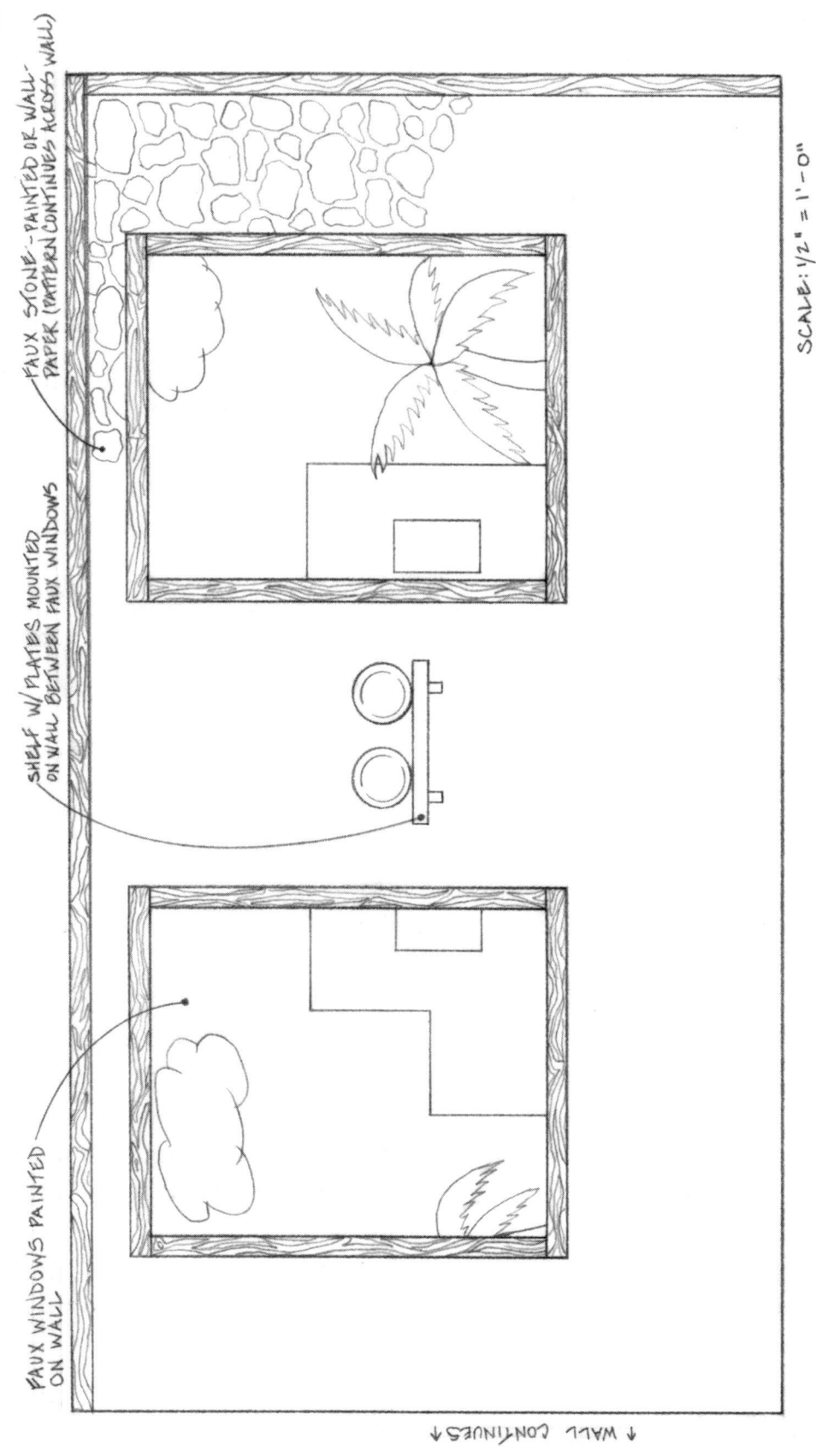

FAUX STONE - PAINTED OR WALLPAPER (PATTERN CONTINUES ACROSS WALL)

SHELF W/ PLATES MOUNTED ON WALL BETWEEN FAUX WINDOWS

FAUX WINDOWS PAINTED ON WALL

SCALE: 1/2" = 1'-0"

↓ WALL CONTINUES ↓

Appendix — page 121

Multi-Use Storage 1

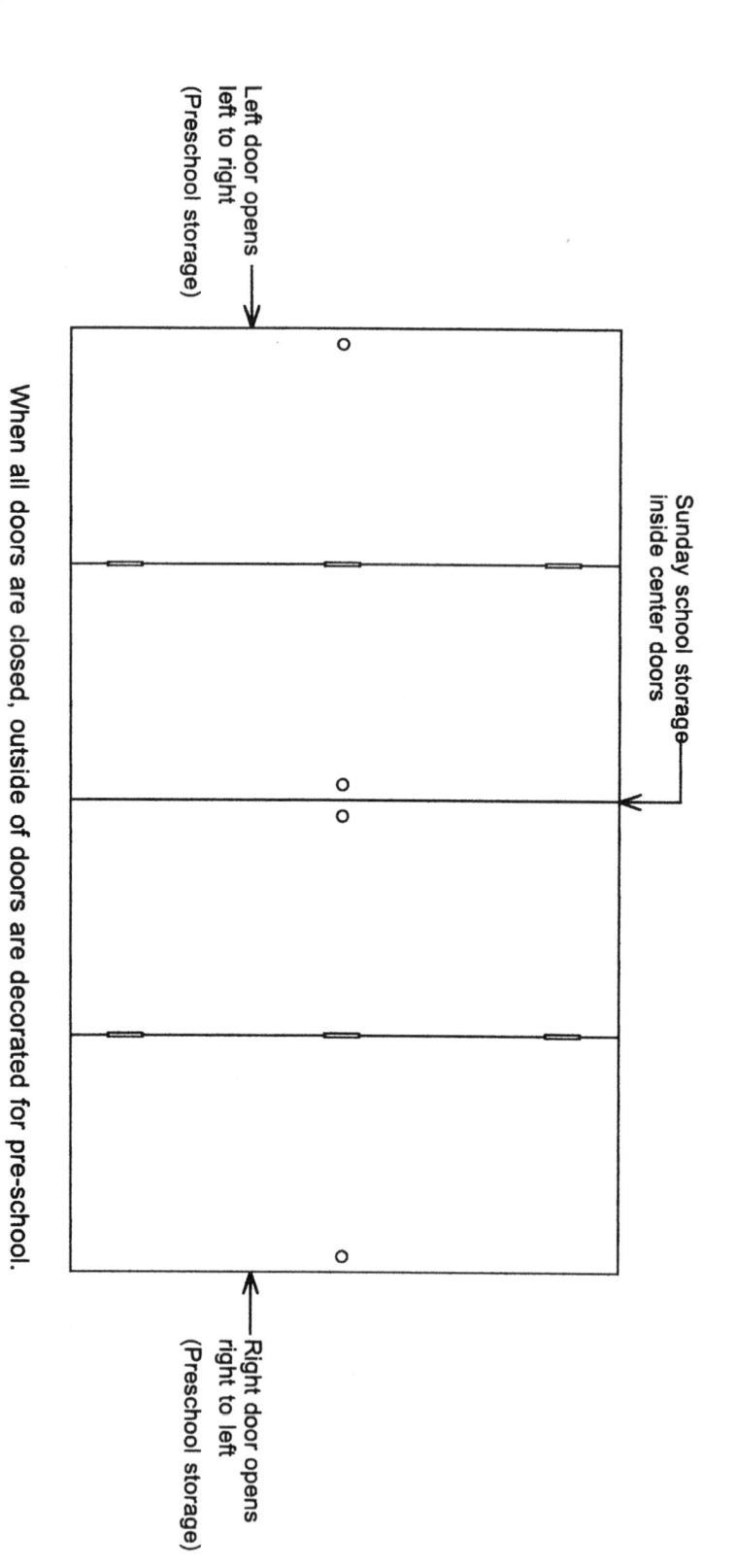

Multi-Use Storage

Left door opens left to right (Preschool storage)

Sunday school storage inside center doors

Right door opens right to left (Preschool storage)

When all doors are closed, outside of doors are decorated for pre-school.

Built-ins for multiple use spaces/shared spaces can work to your advantage. By using the outside and inside of the doors of your storage unit you can change the room for each group. Let's take the example of weekday preschool and Sunday morning church school sharing a room. First, it is best if the ages of both of these groups are similar so furnishings are appropriate for both.

Multi-Use Storage 2

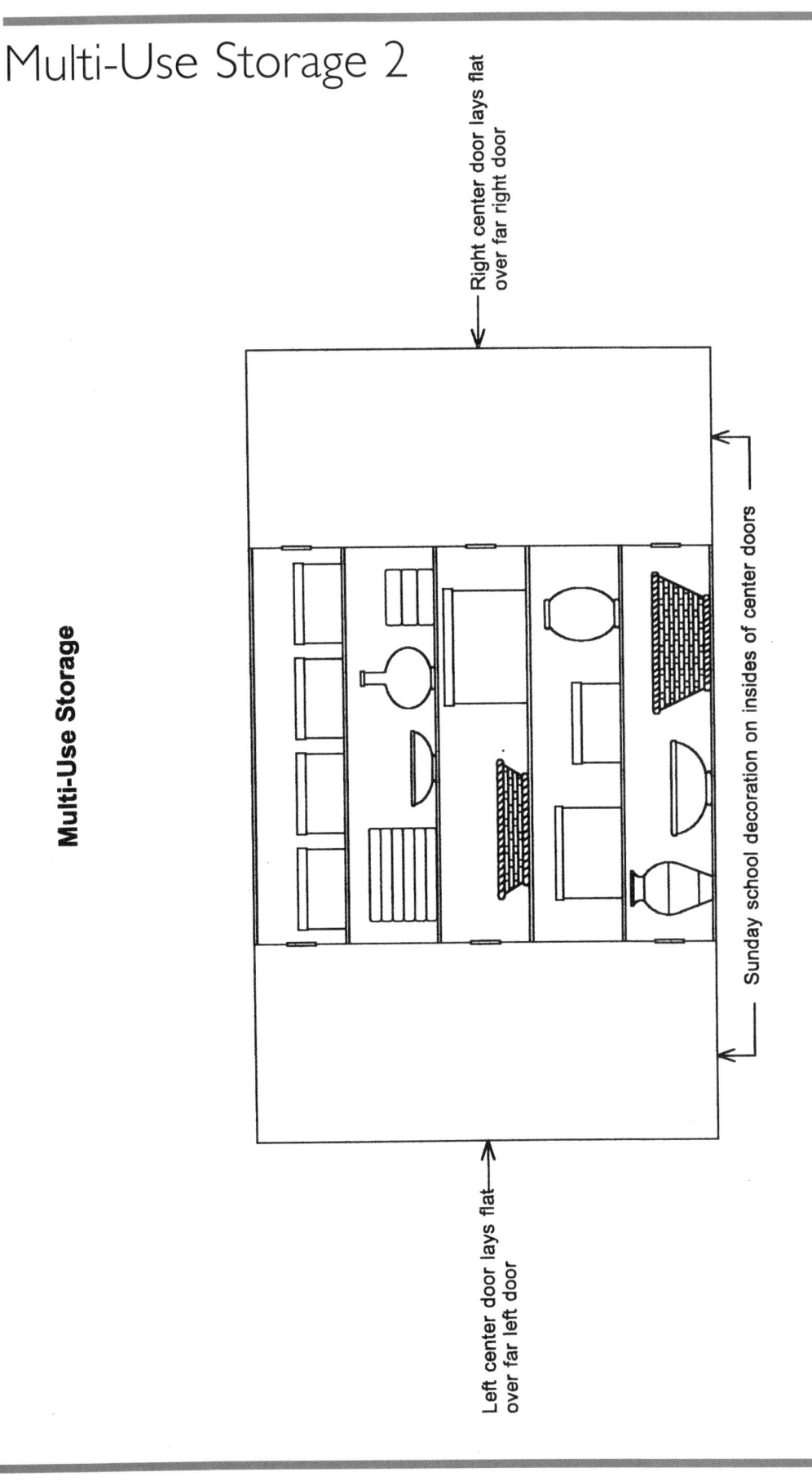

Multi-Use Storage

Right center door lays flat over far right door

Sunday school decoration on insides of center doors

Left center door lays flat over far left door

One group, let's say weekday pre-school, uses the outside of two center doors. The unit is then built with a cabinet on each side of this doublewide cabinet, with single doors on them. The double doors are painted with a motif that identifies the preschool space or has tack board for their activities. The single cabinets on each side will hold their supplies and those single doors will also continue the preschool motif. When the Sunday morning class uses the room, simply open the doors and lay them flat to the right and left. The inside of the doors is now painted the motif for the Sunday school kids and the inside of the open storage holds their supplies.

Appendix   page 123

Room Sign

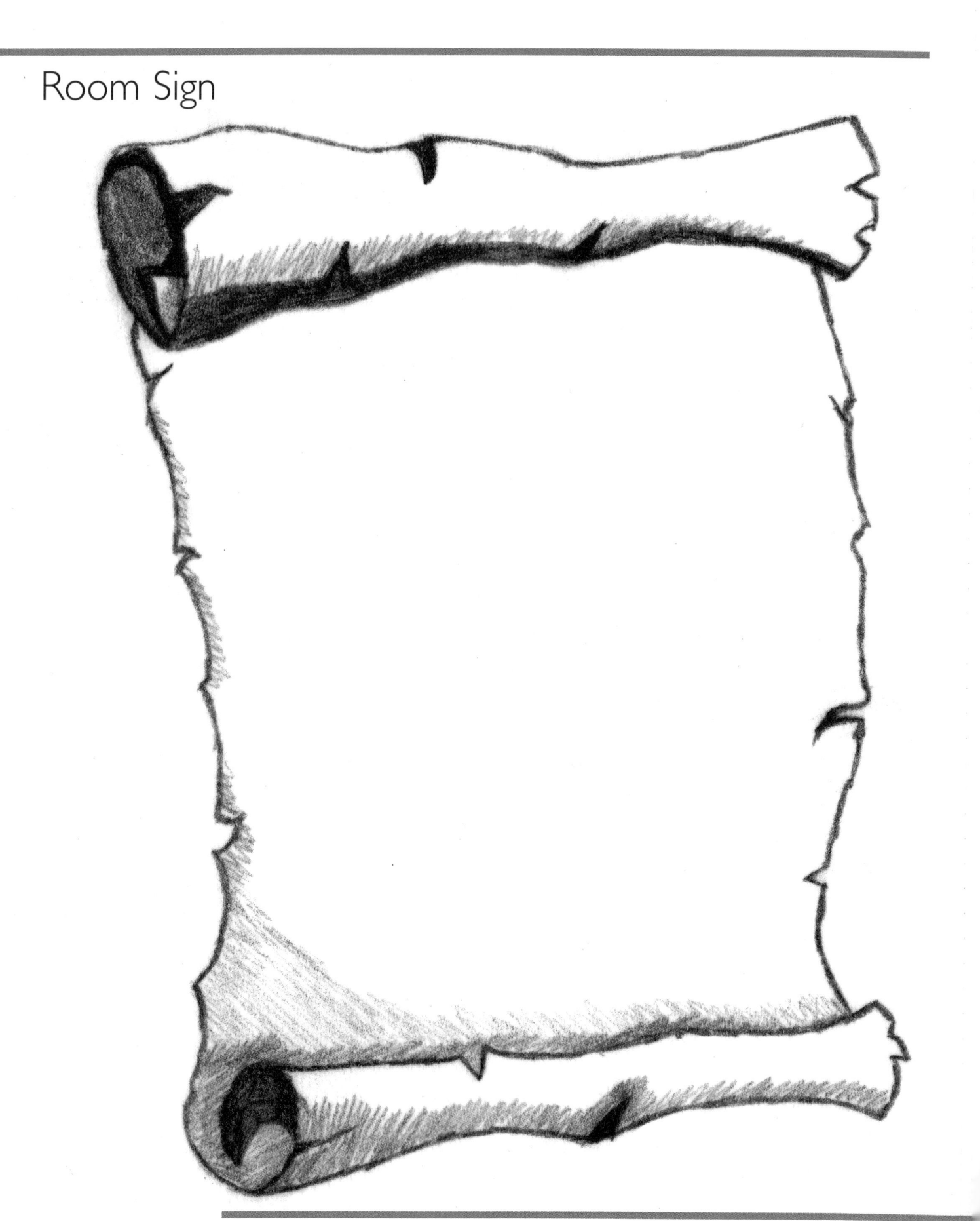

Computer Room 2

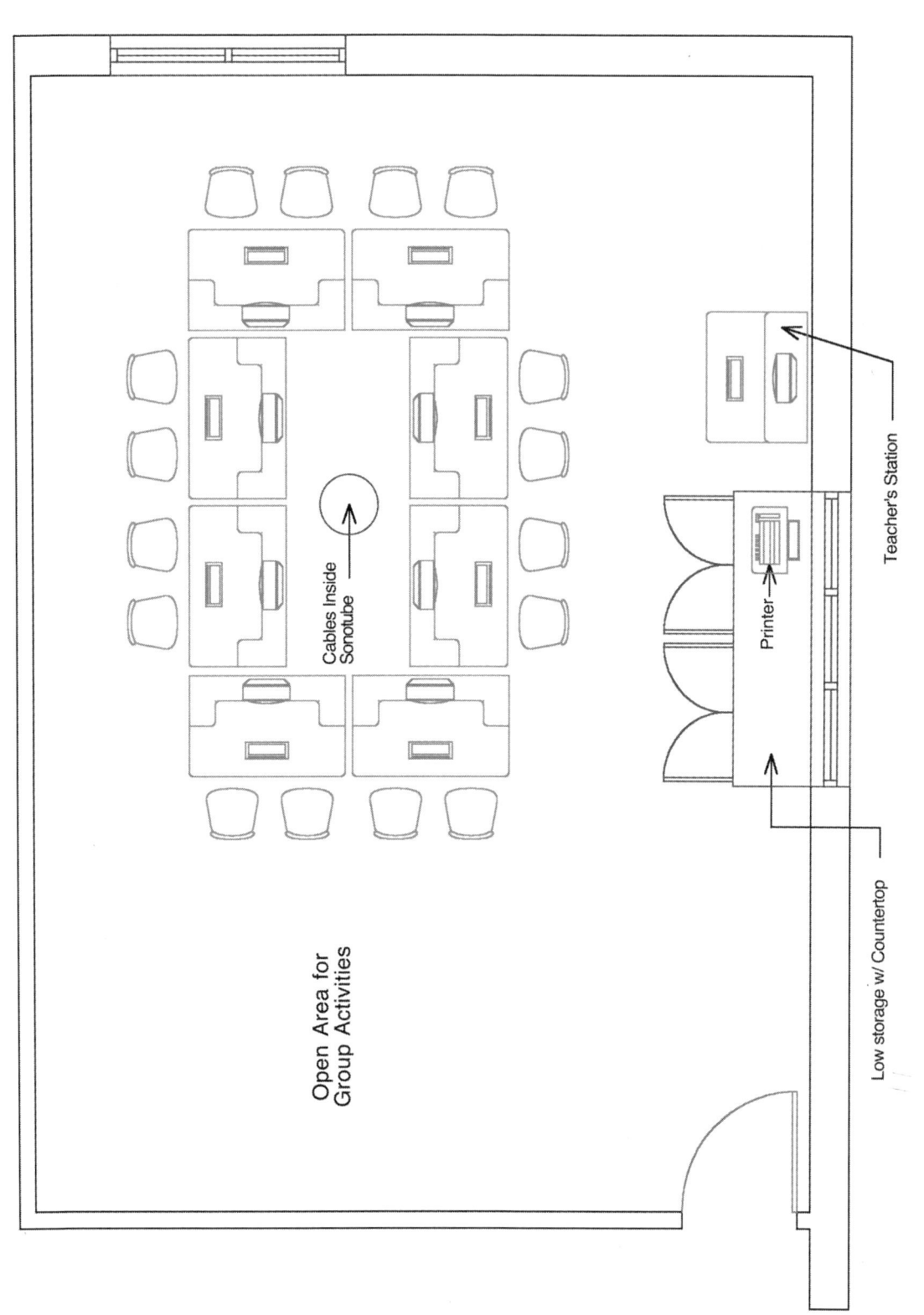

- Teacher's Station
- Printer
- Cables Inside Sonotube
- Low storage w/ Countertop
- Open Area for Group Activities

Appendix page 125

Sunday School isn't about

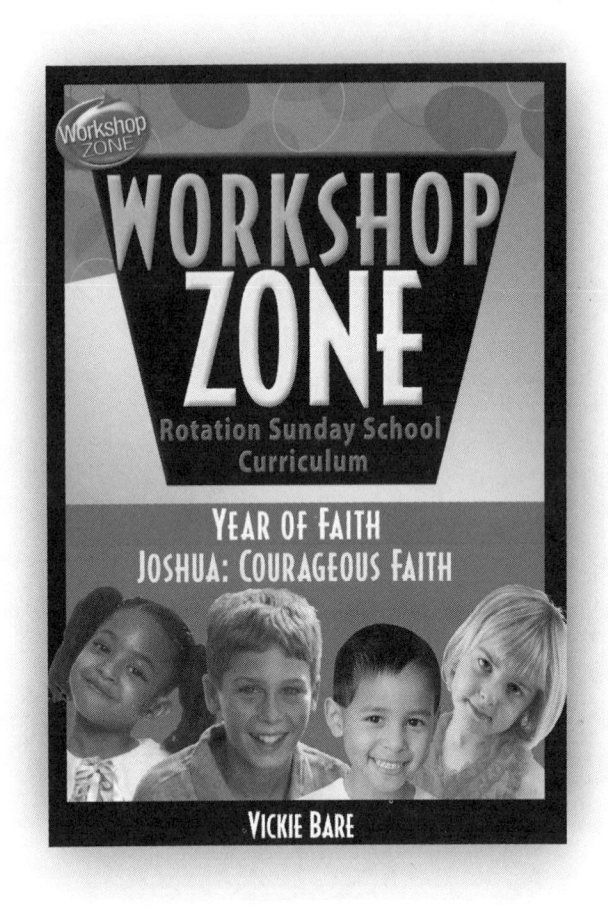

Sunday School has always been about finding the best possible ways to reach children with the life-changing message expressed in God's Word.

Multidimensional/rotation learning is not something entirely new. Rather, it is a fresh paradigm based on our growing understanding of how kids learn. Its purpose is simply to make disciples, as Jesus instructed, by giving kids memorable experiences with the Word.

What drives us to find new, creative ways to present the Bible to kids? Simply this. Each year we learn more and more about how God has programmed us to learn. As we utilize the multiple pathways God has put at our disposal, the impact of our teaching takes on a whole new dynamic. The question before each of us is: "Are we using all the intelligences to convey the message of God's story, to let it sink deep into children's minds and hearts?" Spending weeks on the same story gives children the maximum opportunity to experience the story in ways that will expand their knowledge of God and grow their tender, young faith. So while the workshop rotation model may provide the richest learning environment, there are many ways to be "multidimensional" in teaching God's Word.

Get Your Copy Today! Order Online: www.CookMinistries.com

lectures anymore.

Made up of nine four-week long units, the first year of curriculum, the Year of Faith leads kids in an exploration of different kinds of faith exhibited by key Bible characters.

- 0781442133 - Joshua: Courageous Faith
- 0781442141 - David: Faith vs. Force
- 078144215X - Faith in the Furnace
- 0781442168 - Faith Finds the Messiah
- 0781442176 - Daniel: Faith Faces Lions
- 0781442184 - A Lame Man Healed: Faith Goes Through the Roof
- 0781442192 - Peter: Faith with Wet Feet
- 0781442206 - Resurrection Faith
- 0781442214 - Paul and Silas: Faith in Prison

The 8 workshops in each unit of the Year of Faith are:

Good Shepherd's Inn
Kids settle into a cozy atmosphere and enjoy a Bible storyteller drama, then make and munch a yummy snack that ties in to the story.

Salt and Light Shop
Science and nature exploration leads to wonderful discoveries about our Creator and the stories he gives us to live by.

Mountaintop Productions
The tantalizing smell of popcorn welcomes kids to this workshop where they view and analyze clips that expand the scope of the Bible story.

Faith in Motion
Here's a chance to get rowdy with lively games that challenge kids to recall and relate to important points of the story.

Seaside Studio
For the artist in every child! Kids create personal artistic expressions of their spiritual growth and response to the Bible story.

Stargazer Theater
Let kids be the stars! This workshop sets the stage for Bible study through all kinds of performing arts—puppets, music and drama.

Temple Court
With a focus on spiritual formation, kids openly explore and express their growing faith with real life responses.

Game Zone
Put those growing minds to the test with an interactive Bible story review followed by fun and fascinating game shows such as Holy Word Squares, Bible Jeopardy, Who Wants to Be a Bible Scholar and more!

So, go ahead . . . be daring . . . take your kids on a multidimensional field trip through the Bible . . . and watch them learn!!!

Phone: 1-800-323-7543, Or Visit Your Local Christian Bookstore

The Word at Work... Around the World

What would you do if you wanted to share God's love with children on the streets of your city? That's the dilemma David C. Cook faced in 1870s Chicago. His answer was to create literature that would capture children's hearts.

Out of those humble beginnings grew a worldwide ministry that has used literature to proclaim God's love and disciple generation after generation. Cook Communications Ministries is committed to personal discipleship—to helping people of all ages learn God's Word, embrace his salvation, walk in his ways, and minister in his name.

Opportunities—and Crisis

We live in a land of plenty—including plenty of Christian literature! But what about the rest of the world? Jesus commanded, "Go and make disciples of all nations" (Matt. 28:19) and we want to obey this commandment. But how does a publishing organization "go" into all the world?

There are five times as many Christians around the world as there are in North America. Christian workers in many of these countries have no more than a New Testament, or perhaps a single shared copy of the Bible, from which to learn and teach.

We are committed to sharing what God has given us with such Christians.

A vital part of Cook Communications Ministries is our international outreach, Cook Communications Ministries International (CCMI). Your purchase of this book, and of other books and Christian-growth products from Cook, enables CCMI to provide Bibles and Christian literature to people in more than 150 languages in 65 countries.

Cook Communications Ministries is a not-for-profit, self-supporting organization. Revenues from sales of our books, Bible curriculum, and other church and home products not only fund our U.S. ministry, but also fund our CCMI ministry around the world. One hundred percent of donations to CCMI go to our international literature programs.

CCMI reaches out internationally in three ways:

- Our premier International Christian Publishing Institute (ICPI) trains leaders from nationally led publishing houses around the world to develop evangelism and discipleship materials to transform lives in their countries.

- We provide literature for pastors, evangelists, and Christian workers in their national language. We provide study helps for pastors and lay leaders in many parts of the world, such as China, India, Cuba, Iran, and Vietnam.

- We reach people at risk—refugees, AIDS victims, street children, and famine victims—with God's Word. CCMI puts literature that shares the Good News into the hands of people at spiritual risk—people who might die before they hear the name of Jesus and are transformed by his love.

Word Power—God's Power

Faith Kidz, RiverOak, Honor, Life Journey, Victor, NexGen — every time you purchase a book produced by Cook Communications Ministries, you not only meet a vital personal need in your life or in the life of someone you love, but you're also a part of ministering to José in Colombia, Humberto in Chile, Gousa in India, or Lidiane in Brazil. You help make it possible for a pastor in China, a child in Peru, or a mother in West Africa to enjoy a life-changing book. And because you helped, children and adults around the world are learning God's Word and walking in his ways.

Thank you for your partnership in helping to disciple the world. May God bless you with the power of his Word in your life.

For more information about our international ministries, visit www.ccmi.org.

COOK COMMUNICATIONS MINISTRIES